# THE
# CLAPPER
# MEMO

*General Tilton*
*Thanks!*
*Bob*

## Bob McCarty

ISBN-13: 978-0-615-80803-1
Bob McCarty, L.L.C. Typeset by Heather Justesen
First Edition Printed in the United States of America.

# TABLE OF CONTENTS

# DEDICATION

This book is dedicated to my friend, James L. Chapman, who passed away unexpectedly April 17, 2012, at the age of 69.

The writer of Jim's obituary made note of the fact that the day on which he was born, July 4, suited him well, "because he was a brave Marine who loved his country and was incredibly proud of his service and of all who serve. Jim stood up for what he believed in and devoted his life to helping others."

While the obituary contained a lot of nice words about the man, the conversations I had with him during dozens of phone calls over a three-year period proved those words true.

Jim always seemed to have a story to share. Many came from the days between 1960 and 1966 when he served proudly in the United States Marine Corps, but they weren't the kind of stories told by a man stuck in the moment. Instead, they were shared as a means of communicating keen insights and valuable lessons learned about the human condition.

Though I regret having missed more than one opportunity to meet him in person, I'm thankful I had the chance to work with him in the manner I did.

*Semper fidelis.* Always faithful. The Marine Corp motto describes the man, his relationships, and his commitments.

He is missed.

Semper fi, Jim!

# ABOUT THE TITLE

"Clap on! Clap off! Clap on! Clap off! The Clapper!"

If you're old enough to remember the television commercials that featured those four words repeated over and over again, you can take comfort in the fact that this book has nothing to do with The Clapper®, a sound-activated electrical device introduced to Americans in 1986 as a way to turn lights on and off without reaching for a light switch. Instead, this book has everything to do with shedding light on a subject far more serious that involves a man by the name of James R. Clapper Jr.

Who is Clapper? He's the man President Barack Obama nominated to serve as our nation's fourth Director of National Intelligence (DNI).

Confirmed by the U.S. Senate August 5, 2010, he was sworn in four days later and became both the leader of the U.S. Intelligence Community *and* the principal intelligence advisor to the president of the United States.

Clapper's appointment to the nation's top intelligence post came almost half a century after a less auspicious beginning to his military career as a rifleman in the U.S. Marine Corps Reserve. Eventually, he rose to the three-star rank of lieutenant general in the U.S. Air Force and served as director of the Defense Intelligence Agency (DIA).

Clapper retired from the military in 1995, according to his official biography on the website[1] of the Director of National Intelligence (ODNI), and began working in the private sector for six years, focusing on intelligence-related matters.

Clapper also served as a consultant and advisor to Congress and to the Departments of Defense and Energy as a member of a wide variety of government panels, boards, commissions and advisory groups. In addition, he was a member of the Downing Assessment Task Force that investigated the 1996 terrorist bombing of the Khobar Towers housing complex in Saudi Arabia.

He returned to government service in September 2001 as the first civilian director of the National Imagery and Mapping Agency (NIMA), a unit he transformed into the National Geospatial-Intelligence Agency (NGA) during five years at the helm.

Following his stint at NGA, Clapper served for more than three years in two administrations as the Under Secretary of Defense for Intelligence (USDI). In that role, he served as the principal staff assistant and advisor to the Secretary and Deputy Secretary of Defense (DSD) on intelligence, counterintelligence and security matters for the department. He also doubled as Director of Defense Intelligence (DDI) for DNI.

I had heard of Clapper during my years as a U.S. Air Force public affairs officer (PAO), but it wasn't until 2009 -- the year I launched the investigation that would result in the publication of this book four years later -- that he appeared as a fully-formed blip on my radar screen. It was, in fact, a document from Clapper's office that enabled me, for the first time, to connect some critical "dots" in my investigation.

Though I later found equally-important documents tied to other high-ranking government officials, I could not force myself to go along with recommendations made by well-intentioned friends who said I should change the title "because no one knows who Clapper is."

Fortunately for me, Clapper's name has become more familiar to more Americans in recent years, due largely to a number of headlines related to his actions as DNI.

In response to a question asked by ABC News' Diane Sawyer during an interview[2] December 20, 2010, Clapper appeared to have no knowledge about a group of terrorists who, only days earlier, had been arrested in London.

Two months later, Clapper caught grief for his assessment of the Muslim Brotherhood as a "very heterogeneous group, largely secular." In reality, according to an article[3] published February 10, 2011, at RealClearPolitics.com, the Muslim Brotherhood leans toward strict fundamentalist Islam and, since taking control of Egypt's government after the "Arab Spring," has publicly pushed for Sharia Law to be implemented in the North African country, once a U.S. ally in the region rife with anti-American sentiment.

Most recently, Clapper appeared willing to accept blame for altering Obama Administration talking points[4] produced following the September 11, 2012, attack by elements of Al-Qaeda against the U.S. Consulate in Benghazi, Libya. During that attack, U.S. Ambassador Christopher Stevens was killed along with three others -- Glen Doherty and Tyrone Woods, both former U.S. Navy SEALs, and computer specialist Sean Smith.

While I hope Clapper doesn't continue to make newsworthy gaffes like these, I believe spotlighting his name on this book's cover is appropriate. After reading it, I think you will agree.

# INTRODUCTION

While caught up in the heat of a presidential campaign that ended with Barack Obama becoming the first black man elected president of the United States, I came across an MSNBC.com report[5] by Pulitzer Prize-winning journalist Bill Dedman. Published April 9, 2008, it focused on the U.S. Army's announcement that a new technology, the Preliminary Credibility Assessment Screening System (PCASS), was to be deployed to Iraq and Afghanistan for use by American Soldiers.

After reading Dedman's report, I resisted my initial temptation to write anything serious about the compact offshoot of the polygraph, a technology used by federal agencies since the 1950s.

"It would take too much time away from my coverage of politics," I convinced myself.

When wars were still brewing one year later, however, I decided to revisit PCASS and take a serious look at the devices, referred to by some as "portable polygraphs" or "handheld polygraphs." In short, I wanted to find out what the Department of Defense (DoD) had to say about how PCASS had performed during its first 12 months in war zones.

DoD had, according to Dedman's report, purchased 94 of the devices at a cost of $7,500 each, so I thought the public deserved to know if their investment of tax dollars had paid off in some way (i.e., by helping U.S. forces thwart enemy attacks, capture enemy combatants, obtain valuable intelligence data or something else).

Aside from the public's right to know, I was just plain curious -- and, perhaps, a bit skeptical as well. So I began asking questions.

In separate early-morning emails April 8, 2009, I aimed a handful of questions at Army PAOs inside the Pentagon and at executives of Lafayette Instrument Company, a Lafayette, Indiana-based manufacturer of polygraph machines listed in the article as the Army's source for the PCASS devices.

I asked how many of the initial-purchase PCASS devices had been deployed and into which countries they had been deployed.

Related to that, I asked how frequently they had been used in the field and for details of any Army plans to continue, expand or otherwise modify the use of PCASS devices in the field.

Further, I asked if the use of PCASS been credited with directly saving any American lives or thwarting any enemy operations and if, after one year of use, Army officials considered PCASS effective. If they did, I wanted to know why.

Though not really a question, I ended my inquiry by offering Army officials a chance to provide details of anything else they considered noteworthy about PCASS.

The Army's initial response came 33 minutes after my six questions had arrived in the inbox of Army Lieutenant Colonel Christopher Garver at the Pentagon.

"We'll take a look at this and see if we can find someone to talk to you about it," he replied.

What official answers would I receive? I didn't know for sure, but I had an idea of what to expect.

For instance, I did not expect Army officials to provide answers to two of my questions, because Soldiers who deal with operational issues don't like sharing details like those in public for fear adversaries will discover them. I did, however, expect timely responses to the other questions.

Almost an hour after the Army's initial response, I received a reply via email from Chris Fausett, vice president of polygraph at Lafayette Instrument.

After politely declining to answer my questions, he suggested instead that I contact Deputy Assistant Secretary of Defense for Public Affairs Geoff Morrell, the man serving as press secretary for Secretary of Defense Robert Gates.

"Was this an indication of the level of rapport and influence Fausett and others at Lafayette Instrument had at the Pentagon," I wondered to myself, "or was it an indication of the level of importance the Army had placed on the PCASS project?"

Though doubtful Morrell would want to deal with the matter personally, I fired off a message anyway.

Within two minutes, Morrell responded to my email inquiry, as expected, with a one-line answer: "I recommend you talk with Army Public Affairs."

Little did Morrell know, I was already in contact with the Army.

More than six and one-half hours after Colonel Garver's initial response, I received an email from Dave Foster, an Army civilian PAO.

"Your query is being worked on two fronts with an expectation of a response by mid-day Thursday," Foster wrote.

"I sincerely appreciate your patience as we work to provide you with as much information as we can in response to your query."

Twenty minutes before noon April 9, 2009, I sent a friendly follow-up message, reminding Foster of his "mid-day" promise and asking if he would be providing answers soon.

Eighteen minutes later, Foster offered a measured response, saying he did not anticipate hearing anything from officials at U.S. Central Command (CENTCOM) "until tomorrow at the earliest and perhaps early next week."

Having dealt with all kinds of journalists -- domestic and foreign -- on a frequent and regular basis as an Air Force PAO, I knew what Foster was likely going through as he pushed my questions up the ladder. At the same time, I was acutely familiar with the way things sometimes worked inside the military bureaucracy -- especially at higher levels in the chain of command when questions surfaced about sensitive and/or controversial matters.

The longer I dealt with PAOs at the Pentagon and elsewhere on this set of questions, the more I got the feeling they were facing substantial pressure from people within their respective command structures who did not want to share much information about PCASS. In other words, I got the feeling a pushing-and-pulling process had begun.

Twelve days after my initial contact with the Army, I sent another follow-up message. In it, I asked Foster if I should take the Army's stonewalling as an indication I should resort to filing a federal Freedom of Information Act (FOIA) request. That produced a quick response from Foster in which he indicated he was out of the office to care for an ailing family member.

4

In closing his message, he wrote, "Take such action as you deem appropriate."

Though I had earlier deemed it unnecessary to establish contact with more than one person inside the Army Public Affairs bureaucracy, I decided to abandon Foster and contact Lieutenant Colonel Lee Marvin Packnett, another Army PAO at the Pentagon whose memorable name had been provided by Lafayette Instrument's Fausett as an alternative to his first suggestion, Morrell.

In an email sent to Colonel Packnett just before 11 o'clock that morning, I explained my history of exchanges with Foster and asked him to respond to the same set of PCASS-focused questions that had died on Foster's desk. Soon after, I received a reply in which he told me I should contact Major John Redfield, a U.S. Air Force PAO assigned to CENTCOM.

"Why?" I asked.

"The Army (only bought the equipment). Central Command is the user," Colonel Packnett replied.

By pointing me to CENTCOM, the colonel was pointing me directly to the in-theater folks from whom Foster had been awaiting answers.

A few minutes later, I sent a message to Major Redfield that included essentially the same questions I had sent to Army PAOs at the Pentagon. I received a promising response 11 minutes later.

"I will have to locate the PCASS expert within the headquarters here and see what information I can get," Major Redfield wrote. "I will see if I can get you an update by the close of business today. At the very latest, I will tell you what I have by Tuesday morning (April 21, 2009)."

The major's message left me feeling cautiously optimistic.

At 9:20 the next morning, I received another email from Major Redfield.

"Mr. McCarty, I am still looking for our PCASS expert within the HQ," he advised. "I know who it's not, and that's our biometrics person. I went to him first and he pointed me to our intelligence directorate. If I do not hear back soon from the specific Intel person I was directed to, I will go hunting within the directorate. I realize this still leaves your questions unanswered, but I at least wanted to give you indications of forward momentum."

Two and one-half hours later, a second message arrived from the major.

"Mr. McCarty, I'm in direct contact with the right folks from our Intel directorate to address these questions," Major Redfield explained. "I will do my best to update you this afternoon on when you can anticipate our response. We will be trying to get them as soon as possible, but I'm sure you can understand that there may need to be some internal coordination to be sure we are giving you the most accurate information."

Six hours passed, leading me to suspect Major Redfield was running into resistance in the form of Army brass who did not want to discuss the sensitive subject matter. Then, at five minutes before 5 p.m. Central, I received a message which seemed to indicate Major Redfield might come through after all.

"Mr. McCarty, answers are coming, now that I've got the right source," the major wrote. "I'm just not sure how quickly I will have the response. I don't believe it should be more than a couple of days."

Another update from Major Redfield arrived April 23, 2009.

"Mr. McCarty, I am expecting a response no later than mid-afternoon tomorrow," the major explained. "I understand that you have been attempting to get answers for over two weeks now, but I know that you also realize that I've gotten the questions in front of the right folks only within the past 48 hours."

Yet another message arrived from the major the next day at 4:15 p.m.

"Mr. McCarty, the PCASS folks inform me that they need one more business day to finish coordinating the response. They say they will have it to me by noon on Monday."

I let Major Redfield know I was disappointed in the slow response.

"It's simply taking too long to get answers," I wrote.

Almost three days passed before another message from Major Redfield arrived in the middle of the afternoon.

"Mr. McCarty, I am in the midst of re-typing the response," he wrote. "(Not "re-working" the response, literally re-typing.) Long story...although the response is of course unclassified, the staffing process took place on our classified system, but there's no way to expeditiously transfer the info down from the classified system to the unclassified system. So now I am literally punching away at the keyboard. Shouldn't be much more than 20 minutes."

Three hours passed and another message arrived in my inbox.

"Mr. McCarty, I realize your patience has already worn thin, and I accept full blame for leading you to believe that you would have the information today; that was entirely my fault. Responses to your questions have been formulated, however what remains unresolved is which DoD entity is the proper one to provide you with the information. Unfortunately, it is not as simple as saying that because the device has been used in the CENTCOM area of responsibility, CENTCOM should respond. According to that train of thought, CENTCOM would be commenting on any number of pieces of equipment used in our AOR. Work is continuing on your query, and again any blame for setting misleading expectations on when the information would be forthcoming is mine."

A handful of emails -- including some I sent that were a bit terse -- were exchanged during the next 12 hours. After that, more than a week passed before any more words were exchanged.

Finally, on May 5, 2009, at 9:24 a.m., Major Redfield forwarded a set of what appeared to be carefully-constructed, thoroughly-coordinated answers to the questions I had submitted 27 days earlier.

In response to my question about how many of the initial-purchase PCASS devices were deployed and to which countries they were deployed, Major Redfield wrote, "The Department of the Army went to great lengths to fund the purchase and distribution of PCASS instruments to military organizations conducting operations in Iraq and Afghanistan. The need for this new technology was greatest in those two countries. To the best of CENTCOM's knowledge, all of the initially purchased systems were delivered to units deployed to, or deploying to, those countries."

Regarding frequency of use in the field during the previous year, the major offered a concise explanation.

"Each of the services is responsible for the program management of their combat systems and other equipment," he wrote, "therefore CENTCOM cannot answer this question on frequency of use. For operational security reasons, that information may not be releasable."

When it came to answering my question about plans to continue, expand or modify the use of PCASS, Major Redfield offered a cautious response.

"CENTCOM published guidance which authorizes the use of PCASS in our area of responsibility," he wrote. "The continued use and any expansion of use will be decided by commanders on the ground and those ready to deploy after consultation with their military service leadership. CENTCOM does not envision modifying the use of PCASS, as our current policy permits the use of the device as a screening tool in some very specific situations on specific individuals and under specific conditions. To expose those specifics would endanger the lives of American military personnel."

Had PCASS been credited with saving any American lives or thwarting any enemy operations?

"Unlike a bulletproof vest," he wrote, "PCASS is not a stand-alone tool which one can point to and give credit for saving lives. PCASS is an aid which complements other techniques and is a device which is complemented by other procedures.

"Together these tools have aided intelligence personnel in the identification of locally employed persons who were corresponding with violent extremist organizations, foreign intelligence and security services, and criminal elements," he continued. "There is no way to measure how many lives were saved by taking positive action against individuals who would pass friendly information to persons who would then use that information to attack or attempt to disrupt U.S. and coalition military operations."

Concerning CENTCOM's position on the effectiveness of PCASS, Major Redfield offered comments that caught my attention more than any of the others.

"The comments from forward commanders and their principal intelligence advisors regarding the value of PCASS have been very favorable," he wrote. "In Iraq and Afghanistan, PCASS has proven its value; aiding in the identification of individuals with inimical interests to the U.S. government and our allies has allowed commanders to take actions to reduce the risks these individuals posed."

Regarding my request for "anything else noteworthy about PCASS," the major wrote, "I believe previous responses cover this question."

"So that's it?" I wondered, realizing something was amiss in the answers that, no doubt, had been thoroughly reviewed and edited by senior officials at CENTCOM.

Although I didn't know much about polygraph technology or its portable offshoot at that point, I knew I wasn't receiving complete answers.

Particularly suspect was Major Redfield's reply about the effectiveness of PCASS and his statement about "comments from forward commanders and their principal intelligence advisors regarding the value of PCASS have been very favorable."

What made it stand out was the fact that it conflicted with reports I had already received from the warfighters, active duty and retired, with whom I had also been in contact.

In stark contrast to the official message coming from CENTCOM and, indirectly, from the Pentagon, members of several elite Army and Navy units told me in confidence that they hated PCASS.

In addition, top-level interrogators working at Guantanamo Bay, Baghdad and other locations expressed the same sentiment in letters, official reports and sworn affidavits. Coming from people who put winning wars ahead of defense-contracting politics, the anti-PCASS feedback made me want to learn more. So I did.

During the next four years, I learned more than I ever imagined I might about PCASS and about a newer, non-polygraph technology used in the credibility assessment arena.

Beyond the two technologies, I also became familiar with the people backing each and the lengths to which some of them have been willing to go to win lucrative government contracts.

On one side, I found people who were, for the most part, on the defensive and quick to cite any of several academic studies as proof their technology is superior to all challengers.

On the other, I found people screaming to be heard -- literally and figuratively -- in a situation comparable to one in which a medical researcher discovers a cure for cancer but is ignored by the medical community. Why? Because his cure threatens the professional livelihoods of individuals (i.e., doctors, research scientists et al) purportedly seeking a cure for the affliction.

In between, I found people with years of hands-on experience using both technologies. Not surprisingly, they seemed most objective in their analyses.

Most surprising, perhaps, was my realization that the people backing these two competing technologies are merely the latest recruits in a battle -- no, let's call it a "turf war" -- that's been raging quietly and mostly out of public view for more than 40 years.

\* \* \*

*THE CLAPPER MEMO* reveals never-before-published details from the battlefield, gleaned from scores of interviews, hundreds of documents and assorted correspondence, and numerous inquiries made to government agencies -- most at the federal level.

People from all walks of life shared insights, insider information and occasional doses of insanity related to their personal experiences as veterans in this turf war.

People from across the United States as well as around the world -- in places like Afghanistan, Cuba, Iraq and Mexico -- shared.

During scheduled and unscheduled interviews. Through official and unofficial channels. By phone calls and email message. By Facebook and Twitter messages. Even by "snail mail." They shared.

Most told the truth. Others did not.

Some were forthcoming with information while others forced me to use legal means, such as FOIA and various state "sunshine" and Open Records laws, to flush out answers.

When all else failed, I turned to old-fashioned detective work.

In many instances throughout this book, you'll find names have been changed or omitted entirely in an effort to protect individuals for reasons that should become apparent as you read.

After reading this book, parts of which read like a soap opera storyline, I hope you walk away with a clear understanding that, as long as this turf war continues unabated, American Soldiers and citizens alike remain at greater-than-necessary risk of becoming victims.

# CHAPTER ONE:
## 'Green-on-Blue'

Even those who pay scant attention to the daily news have likely heard about the "Green-on-Blue" attacks taking place in Afghanistan.

Insidious by nature, each attack involves at least one Afghan who, while serving in an official capacity as a uniform-wearing member of an Afghan government organization (i.e., military, police or security), turns against the very foreigners alongside whom he works and/or trains.

Often, the attacks involve the use of small arms fire and. On occasion, however, they take the form of suicide attacks or involve the use of improvised explosive devices (IEDs) and/or other deadly measures.

Though the people behind the attacks target Americans more often than those of other nationalities, they remain willing to kill others -- even Afghans -- with whom they disagree. "Equal opportunity killers" seems an apt description.

When it comes to the colorful label initially applied to the attacks, "green" refers to supposedly-friendly members of the Afghan National Security Force (ANSF) and Afghan Security Group (ASG), and "blue" the color associated with members of the International Security Assistance Force (ISAF) members (a.k.a., "the good guys").

For some six years now, reports about Green-on-Blue attacks in Afghanistan have surfaced in the news on a regular basis -- sometimes daily -- in the United States. One of those attacks took place March 19, 2011.

* * *

At approximately 8 a.m., members of 4th Squadron, 2nd Stryker Cavalry Regiment (4/2 SCR TAC) were cleaning their weapons while gathered around their Stryker armored fighting vehicles outside the Tactical Operations Center (TOC) at Forward Operating Base (FOB) Frontenac, located about 20 minutes north of Kandahar by helicopter.

It wasn't their usual place for cleaning weapons, but the Soldiers had been told they had additional time to prepare for a mission that would take them outside the confines of the ISAF outpost in the Arghandab River valley north of Kandahar. So they cleaned. Out in the open. Ramps down. Inside the entry-controlled environment of the FOB.

At about the same time, a convoy of large and colorful "jingle trucks" arrived at the FOB.

Commonly used by contractors in Afghanistan and Pakistan and known for the jingle sound made by chains hanging from their bumpers, the customized vehicles were received at the entry control point and escorted to a container area next to the TOC.

Those doing the escorting that day were employees of Tundra Security Group, a private security company (PSC) based in Canada, who had been hired to provide both base defense security and a Quick Reaction Force (QRF) at the FOB.

Soon after the jingle trucks arrived, 4/2 members found themselves under attack.

At 19 minutes after the hour, according to the 14-page Army Regulation 15-6 Investigation Report[6] produced April

14, 2011, an armed Afghan employee of Tundra moved toward the American Soldiers, drew his weapon and began shooting at the Soldiers.

Facing what was described as "well-aimed automatic fire," the majority of Soldiers immediately dropped to the ground and began seeking cover toward the front ends of their vehicles. With their weapons disassembled for cleaning, most had no immediate means to defend themselves.

Two soldiers -- a specialist and a captain -- took actions that would be highlighted in the report.

Upon realizing he and his fellow Soldiers were under attack, the specialist -- who had his weapon assembled, but not loaded -- immediately moved between the Strykers and some nearby T-Walls (a.k.a., "Bremer walls"). Once behind a section of the 12-foot-high, portable, steel-reinforced walls, he began loading his weapon.

At the same time, the Afghan continued firing, expending all of his rounds as he moved deliberately around the vehicles toward where the remaining Soldiers had sought cover. Then he reloaded and continued his approach toward those Soldiers.

Before the Afghan could fire another shot, however, he came into the field of view of the specialist who, with his gun now assembled and loaded, fired a well-aimed shot.

Though the Afghan assailant's body armor kept that shot from doing damage, it didn't stop the shots that followed -- into his hip, shoulder and head -- and dropped the man to the ground.

And it didn't stop the final shot, fired by the captain when he saw the Afghan still moving, still posing a threat.

Despite the heroic actions of the American Soldiers described above, two of the unit's men -- Corporal Donald

Mickler, 29, a native of Dayton, Ohio, and Private First Class Rudy Acosta, 19, of Santa Clarita Valley, California -- died from injuries they suffered during the attack. Four others were injured.

Also killed that day was the Afghan assailant, a Tundra employee, Shia Ahmed.

Ahmed's coworkers later described him as having been a reserved, quiet individual who had revealed no clear indications prior to the attack that he was about to do anything, according to the report.

During the weeks following the attack, the investigating officer -- an Army major whose name, like the other Soldiers who survived the attack, was redacted from the copy of the investigation report I obtained -- learned Ahmed had a history of animosity toward American Soldiers. A history that included using aliases.

"Most significant," the major wrote on page one of his report, "Shia Ahmed had expressed intentions to target US Soldiers."

Deeper into his report, the investigating officer pointed out several flaws in the process via which Afghans like Ahmed were vetted (i.e., screened) prior to working alongside American and other coalition forces (CF) personnel.

In addition, he described some of the policies defining duties and responsibilities for vetting as "vague and confusing."

In the final section of his report, the investigating officer used a half-dozen paragraphs to recommend "a larger comprehensive investigation be initiated to examine the vetting and screening procedures across Afghanistan."

\* \* \*

During a phone conversation some 16 months after the death of his son Rudy, Dante Acosta told me it had taken Army officials until December -- almost nine months after the official investigation report was completed -- to provide him a copy.

Why such a long delay? Perhaps because some Army officials -- and, likely, DoD officials as well -- didn't want to make public any details about the slipshod process being used to vet Afghans. After all, it might upset folks back home -- including the relatives and friends of the two fallen Soldiers who became victims of the flawed vetting process.

I wasn't surprised to hear about the long delay experienced by Mr. Acosta. After all, I had already experienced what it's like to wait a long time for answers from the Pentagon, and more waiting was in my future.

# CHAPTER TWO:
# The Vetting Process

More than a year after the Green-on-Blue attack at FOB Frontenac, I began asking follow-up questions having to do with both PCASS and the process by which uniform-wearing Afghans who serve alongside American and CF personnel were being vetted. *NOTE: At the time I asked these questions, I had not yet read the investigation report about the attack at FOB Frontenac.*

On March 27, 2012, I forwarded a list of nine questions to PAOs at DIA and ISAF. Most of the replies I received came within two weeks; others took up to a month.

Via those replies, I learned Army units were still receiving PCASS training at the National Center for Credibility Assessment (NCCA) at Fort Jackson, South Carolina.

In addition, I learned from Lieutenant Colonel Tom Veale, an Army PAO assigned to DIA, that NCCA had, as of April 2012, provided PCASS training to more than 2,500 students from all branches of the U.S. military; 70 percent of those trained were from the Army; and not a single student had ever failed the course.

Somewhat surprisingly, I learned that refinements had been made to PCASS since it was first deployed to the field in 2008, but none of those refinements had affected the performance of the technology.

Further, I learned PCASS was still being used, along with about 10 other tools, to screen applicants for positions on U.S. bases and some NATO bases in Afghanistan.

Finally, I learned neither ISAF nor U.S. forces were responsible for vetting Afghans serving in either the Afghan National Army (ANA) or Afghan National Police (ANP), according to Lieutenant Colonel Jimmie E. Cummings, an ISAF PAO.

Regarding the last point above, Colonel Cummings explained that Afghans use an eight-step process in vetting their candidates and that I should direct my question (i.e., the one about whether or not PCASS had been used to screen any Afghan military or law enforcement personnel who, later, went on to attack U.S. military personnel) to Sediq Sediqqi, a spokesperson for the Afghan Ministry of Interior (MoI).

I took the colonel's advice and forwarded three questions to the Afghan official April 13, 2012.

My first question was broad in scope: "What tools, methods and/or procedures have been used by the Afghan government to screen ANSF members in an attempt to determine their loyalty and/or trustworthiness?"

My second question was specific: "Is any form of polygraph technology being used to screen ANSF members in an attempt to determine their loyalty and/or trustworthiness? If so, please describe."

My third and final question was more sensitive: "Were any of the ANSF members who have been implicated in the shootings of Americans subjected to screening prior to their involvement in the shootings? If so, did they successfully pass those screenings? Details please."

Though Sediqqi politely acknowledged receipt of my questions and wrote in a same-day reply, "we will get back to you as soon as possible," he never got back to me. In fact, he ignored multiple follow-up attempts I made over a period of several months.

While engaged in asking questions about the vetting process, I came across three other sources of related information.

One good source was a NATO Media Backgrounder[7]. Dated March 2011, it contained a description of the eight-step vetting process Colonel Cummings had mentioned.

"Recruitment is now following an 8-step vetting process," the description began. "Upon signing the enlistment contract agreement, the recruit must get two individuals (village elder, Mullah, or other local government representative) to sign and vouch for the recruit. These individuals are held responsible if any discrepancy in the contract is found. The recruit's paperwork and government ID is reviewed and basic biometric information (retinal scan, fingerprints, height, age, and weight) is collected, added to the recruit's personnel file and accompanies the recruit to training. The biometric data is then checked to see if the individual has any known criminal or insurgent links. Approximately 6% of applicants are screened out for either drug use or medical conditions."

Any objective analysis of those eight steps reveals serious flaws.

For instance, a recruit with anti-American views can subvert the process simply by getting two Mullahs (i.e., clergy) -- individuals who might share his radical views -- to sign papers and vouch for him.

When it comes to the biometric collection steps that are part of the vetting process, it's not a stretch to believe that a person willing to die for his cause (i.e., a suicide bomber) might regard the requirement to provide biometric data as a minor inconvenience that, once completed, simply allows him greater access to his target(s).

Finally, the likelihood that an applicant's records, identification papers and biometric data will yield links to records of his criminal activity or insurgent involvement remains very slim in the Stone Age country where, according to government and press reports too numerous to mention, record-keeping is suspect at best and corruption runs deep.

Moving on.

A second source of information about the eight-step vetting process was the transcript[8] of the testimony of U.S. Marine Corps General John R. Allen before the U.S. Senate Armed Services Committee March 22, 2012.

Not only did the ISAF commander address Green-on-Blue casualty figures and convey that he was genuinely concerned about bringing an end to the unconventional attacks, but he also mentioned the existence of a third source of information -- an unclassified Army handbook about the fratricide-murder phenomenon -- from which I thought I might learn more about the vetting process he told senators had been used for "months." Immediately, I set out to obtain a copy of it.

In a FOIA request filed April 10, 2012, I asked officials at the U.S. Army FOIA Office at Fort Belvoir, Virginia, to send me a copy of the Army handbook -- published under the title, "Inside the Wire Threats - Afghanistan," and marked "For Official Use Only."

Upon receipt, the folks at Fort Belvoir forwarded my request to officials at Fort Leavenworth, Kansas, home to the document's publisher, the Army Centers for Army Lessons Learned (CALL) -- a sort of military think tank.

Per federal law, I expected to wait 20 days for a determination by CALL officials as to whether they would release the document to me. At worst, I figured the Army might cite "extenuating circumstances" and request an extra ten days, also allowed by law, before responding to my request.

Many messages were exchanged, and many phone calls made, but my FOIA request languished in limbo without any determination for three months.

Then, on July 25, 2012, I received an update from Anastasia Kakel, records administrator at the Army's Training and Doctrine Command (TRADOC) at Fort Eustis, Virginia. She confirmed she had received my FOIA packet from officials at Fort Leavenworth twice.

The first time, she sent it back for more information, she explained. After receiving it a second time, she told me she anticipated the process to take another two weeks.

If her estimate proved accurate, I would receive a determination by August 8, 2012 -- Day 120 of my quest! One day before that milestone date arrived, however, I received more news about the status of my FOIA request.

Kakel explained that she expected to receive a legal review "in the next few days and then anticipate processing it to DOD FOIA Office for their review."

A curious statement followed.

"At this time, I can't estimate how long it will take," she wrote, "as this is the first time we are processing a FOIA request this way."

In other words, according to Kakel, my request was setting some sort of a precedent. Perhaps, I *was* on to something?

Kakel's statement left me wondering why Army officials were so reluctant to release a copy of the handbook -- even after I told them at one point during the time-consuming affair I would accept a redacted version in place of no version at all.

Before Army and DoD officials made any determination, however, my FOIA request grabbed the attention of someone who apparently had access to the document I had sought for so long. That someone sent me a copy of it -- all 42 pages (not including the front and back covers).

Not experienced in the conduct of wars against insurgents, I'm not one to divulge much in the way of the handbook's contents. I will, however, confirm that the handbook did include an explanation of the eight-step vetting process mentioned by Colonel Cummings and General Allen and contained in the NATO Media Backgrounder.

What I learned during the lengthy process of trying to get a copy of the handbook (i.e., that ISAF officials were not comfortable answering questions about the process used to vet Afghans) turned out to be more valuable than any of the "Observations, Insights, and Lessons" the handbook's cover promised were inside.

* * *

After a Green-on-Blue attack July 3, 2012, left five U.S. troops in Afghanistan wounded, another ISAF spokesperson seemed quick to put an official "spin" on the incident. At the same time, however, he appeared to reveal ISAF officials had changed their approach and were getting more involved in efforts to stop these attacks.

Evidence of the apparent change in ISAF's approach to combating the attacks appeared in the fifth paragraph of a *Stars and Stripes* article[9] published July 4, 2012 -- *after* Lieutenant Commander Brian Badura was reported to have said the number of attacks against U.S. and coalition troops by ANSF members was low relative to the number of Afghan troops and police working with ISAF forces.

"First and foremost, ISAF is getting together with our Afghan National Security Partners on the vetting and process they use," the PAO told *Stripes*. "What we're trying to do is make sure that any of the mitigation does not damage the trust we've built between the ANSF and coalition units."

Notice the active verb, *is*, used twice in that paragraph.

Soon after reading the article, I asked Colonel Cummings, via email, to describe what was taking place during this "getting together" process mentioned by Commander Badura and to provide details about who was involved on the U.S. forces side of the table.

In addition, I asked him when the "getting together" process had begun, if a timeline for completing the process had been established and if, to date, the process had resulted in any significant changes in the way Afghans were being vetted.

After writing in his reply that little had changed since our discussion three months earlier about the ways ISAF officials advise Afghans, Colonel Cummings addressed the eight-step vetting process again.

"The 8-step vetting process, which we have discussed in the past, is the result of our advising on this issue. Just like everything else that we (ISAF) advise on in Afghanistan, it is an ongoing and continuous process. We continually advise our Afghan partners on ways to improve processes. Again, the

Afghans have the lead and are responsible for vetting their recruits into their security forces."

New developments related to my inquiry began surfacing 31 days later when top brass began engaging in semantics rather than taking real steps toward combating the Green-on-Blue problem.

Army General Martin E. Dempsey, chairman of the Joint Chiefs of Staff, was quoted in a CNN report[10] August 14, 2012, as saying the "Green-on-Blue" label is a misnomer.

"I think you'll hear us start talking about these incidents more as 'insider attack,' rather than green-on-blue, because what that does is it understates the effect that this is having on the ANSF itself," he said.

That statement was made on the same day Generals Dempsey and Allen launched a top-down public relations campaign to rebrand the incidents as "insider" attacks, telling all who would listen that the "Green-on-Blue" label understated the fact that Afghans are "suffering from the same … trend that we're suffering from."

On August 20, 2012, the generals used a show of force -- or, in this case, stars -- to communicate the message that they had placed a high level of importance on finding a way to reduce the number of attacks.

Generals Dempsey and Allen met in Kabul, Afghanistan, with Marine Corps General James N. Mattis, CENTCOM commander, to discuss the matter of Green-on-Blue attacks and pose for photos with the troops.

Knowing that three four-star generals had gotten together, in person and publicly, to say they were working on developing a "fix" for the problem left me convinced, beyond a shadow of a doubt, that the eight-step process was not working.

That same day, two Bloomberg reporters cited George Little, chief Pentagon spokesperson, as the source of a statement about Afghan security ministries' efforts to combat Green-on-Blue attacks.

According to their article[11], Little said Afghan security ministries had adopted more "rigorous vetting procedures" for Afghans seeking to join the security forces.

After reading the article, I asked Air Force Major Lori Hodge, Colonel Cummings' replacement at ISAF, to explain exactly what kind of "rigorous vetting procedures" had been adopted and what made the new procedures different from previously-followed ones.

I received a reply within 24 hours.

"In response to your question on the vetting procedures adopted by the Afghans," Major Hodge wrote, "the Afghan National Security Force is working hard to make their vetting processes more robust."

As examples of the measures being taken, she explained that ANSF had introduced re-vetting procedures for ANA soldiers returning from leave, outlawed the sale of uniforms, and established an anonymous reporting system.

Further, the major explained that Afghan President Hamid Karzai had issued a presidential decree which mandates that ANA recruits be interviewed by a four-person council consisting of officials from the Ministries of Defense (MoD) and MoI as well as the National Directorate of Security (NDS) and medical department officials.

In closing, Major Hodge reiterated what her predecessor had told me April 4, 2012, and July 4, 2012, before referring me to MoD officials for further information on vetting procedures.

"While we advise our Afghan counterparts," she wrote, "the vetting of recruits and personnel is an Afghan-led and - owned process and they would be the appropriate authorities to discuss it in more detail."

Having realized zero success to date in obtaining answers from officials inside the Afghan government, officially known as the Government of the Islamic Republic of Afghanistan (GIRoA), I didn't attempt to make contact with MoI's Sediqqi or any of his Afghan colleagues again.

Three days after my most-recent electronic conversation with Major Hodge, General Allen held a media videoconference at the Pentagon.

Speaking from Afghanistan, he told reporters he suspected the recent increase in Green-on-Blue attacks may have had something to do with asking Afghans involved in those attacks to perform dangerous operations during the recent Muslim holy month, Ramadan. The general's comments – which, at best, sounded like an "educated guess" -- drew widespread criticism but little else.

After two weeks passed, I came across news that prompted me to ask another series of questions that had the effect of putting ISAF officials back on the spot.

Contrary to everything I had been told to date by ISAF PAOs about who was responsible for vetting Afghans, I had it confirmed -- by Major Hodge via email -- that U.S. Special Operations Forces were in charge of vetting Afghan Local Police (ALP) recruits.

She confirmed that fact for me after I presented her with a statement contained in the opening paragraph of a September 4, 2012, news report[12] in which freelance reporter John Wendle described U.S. Army troops as being "in charge of the interview" of an Afghan recruit and "getting increasingly frustrated" with the vetting process.

In addition to offering the confirmation, Major Hodge apologized for having omitted such an important detail from her earlier correspondence with me.

When pressed later that month for answers to two of my toughest questions, Major Hodge offered two less-than-helpful recommendations.

My question about whether or not PCASS was being used to screen any Afghan recruits prompted her, once again, to recommend I contact someone in the Afghan government — this time, at MoD.

My interest in learning whether or not any Afghans who had undergone PCASS screening proceeded to wage Green-on-Blue attacks prompted the major to recommend I seek answers by filing a FOIA request. The subject of my questioning, after all, had to do with "results of investigations," she said.

Based on my record of success -- or lack thereof -- in obtaining information via FOIA, I decided to leave those questions unanswered. After all, I *was* in the middle of a turf war and had more battles to cover.

# CHAPTER THREE:
## 'Turf War'

To understand the origins of this turf war, one must travel back in time to 1971, some three years after Lieutenant Colonel Allan D. Bell Jr. retired from the Army; more than 20 years after he had returned from the Korean Peninsula; and nearly six decades after Harvard graduate student William Moulton Marston[13] (a.k.a., "Charles Marston") began working on a blood pressure-related approach to detecting deception in 1915.

As the war in Vietnam was winding down amidst much vocal opposition at home, Colonel Bell and two colleagues -- Wilson H. Ford and Charles R. McQuiston -- began marketing a new investigative technology they had developed as a tool to detect levels of significant emotional stress from voice utterances.

A former intelligence officer, Colonel Bell envisioned many uses for the technology but believed it held the most promise as a tool for use in psychological and psychiatric evaluations and in lie detection -- perhaps as a replacement for the often-controversial polygraph. Convincing others, he soon realized, would be an uphill battle.

For ten years after introducing the new technology to the market, Colonel Bell and his colleagues received the cold-shoulder treatment from influential people inside the often-overlapping circles of academia, government, and industry.

Understanding the Cold War-like situation in which he and his colleagues found themselves, Colonel Bell addressed what was at stake in an article[14] published in the March 1981 issue of the American Society of Industrial Security (ASIS) publication, *Security Management.*

He began by pointing out several important differences between the polygraph and his company's new technology.

Among the differences, the colonel explained, was that his technology dealt with absolute stress levels while polygraph was capable only of displaying relative stress levels.

In addition, his technology did not require the attachment of sensors and, thereby, eliminated stress caused by the unnatural and sometimes-painful physical constraints of polygraph attachments, he added.

Finally, the colonel explained, responses evaluated by his technology were essentially instantaneous while those evaluated by the polygraph were derived from the end of a chain of body-chemistry actions and reactions.

With those differences spelled out, Colonel Bell went on to share his belief that the development of his technology was forcing polygraph professionals to consider three difficult options as they weighed plans for the future.

Their first option, he explained, was to accept the new technology and change over to it, realizing such a change would involve scrapping polygraph equipment and purchasing the new technology.

In lieu of that, they could attempt to continue with the polygraph and hope for the best, realizing this course would probably result in the "slow death" of the polygraph.

As a last resort, the colonel wrote, they could attempt to ensure the survival of the polygraph by eliminating the challenger. And that's what they did.

"The polygraph professional leadership reportedly selected the third course of action, which was not necessarily an illogical choice," Colonel Bell wrote, noting that polygraph loyalists would ensure the survival of their preferred technology if the new technology "could be nipped in the bud."

Though Colonel Bell's company changed hands over the years and has yet to make deep inroads as a polygraph competitor, another company was able to elevate its game to the point where its truth-verification product became the leading challenger to polygraph.

That company is the West Palm Beach, Florida-based National Institute for Truth Verification (NITV), founded by Charles Humble. Its product is the Computer Voice Stress Analyzer® (CVSA®).

Rather than offer an infomercial pitchman-style description of CVSA® as the "new and improved version of Colonel Bell's technology," I'll simply report what I've learned about CVSA®.

It comes packaged in the form of proprietary software loaded on a laptop computer and includes a unique automatic-scoring algorithm its backers say eliminates the examiner bias often cited as a polygraph flaw.

Unlike the polygraph, however, it requires no wires, blood-pressure cuffs or other components with which an interrogation subject must maintain any form of contact during an exam.

Perhaps the most important difference between the polygraph and CVSA®, according to NITV officials, is that the latter device was never intended to -- and is not expected to -- accomplish stress measurements in "game" situations. Instead, CVSA® is designed specifically to detect the levels of stress encountered in real-world applications and not in laboratory scenarios where those being interviewed face no real jeopardy.

At the time of this book's publication, CVSA® was the most-widely-used non-polygraph investigative technology on the market, used by examiners at more than 2,000 law enforcement agencies worldwide, 90 percent of which are in the United States.

Many of the agencies that purchased the original analog version of the technology during the late 1980s upgraded to the digital version when it became available in 1997.

As a result of its success, especially since the dawn of the new millennium, CVSA® stands as the primary target of polygraph loyalists who have embraced Colonel Bell's aforementioned third option (i.e., eliminating the challenger).

\* \* \*

A large number of polygraph loyalists can be found among the ranks of military and civilian employees of the U.S. Army. This is largely a result of the Secretary of the Army being designated DoD's executive agent for polygraph training in 1985.

Though tempted to share a 1,500-word history of the federal polygraph infrastructure that's available for all to read on an Uncle Sam-owned and -managed website[15], I offer a condensed version that's both accurate and more palatable:

The federal government's primary polygraph training organization dates back to 1951 when it was known as the U.S. Army Polygraph School. Since then, it has been physically relocated twice, organizationally relocated three times and had its name changed three times since 1961. Today, it's known as NCCA.

In addition to mentioning it in the condensed history above, I must note that the organization known originally as the U.S. Army Polygraph School will receive several additional mentions, under different names, beyond this point. More important than remembering any of those changing names, however, is realizing that each of them -- Department of Defense Polygraph Institute (DoDPI), the Defense Academy for Credibility Assessment (DACA) and NCCA -- can more simply be referred to as "Polygraph Headquarters."

On several occasions throughout the remainder of this book, I'll use that two-word descriptor to identify the organization whose influence -- if that can be determined by the output of its graduates -- has grown dramatically.

According to a DoD report[16], polygraph examiners throughout the entire federal government conducted approximately 8,000 polygraph exams between October 1, 1999, and September 30, 2000. Then, almost one year later, the history-changing attacks of September 11 took place.

During the 10 years that followed those attacks, the number of polygraph exams conducted within the federal government skyrocketed. According to a USDI report[17] covering the 12-month period ending April 30, 2011, DoD polygraph examiners alone conducted more than 43,000 polygraph exams.

The number of polygraph exams conducted wasn't the only thing to increase during the dozen years after September 11, 2001.

Perhaps sensing the need to "strike while the iron was hot," officials at the Chattanooga, Tennessee-based American Polygraph Association (APA) launched an all-out assault on voice-stress technologies, including CVSA®, within months of the attacks. The assault began when the MARCH/APRIL 2002 edition of *APA Newsletter*[18] was mailed to APA members.

Included in that edition was a message in which Milton O. "Skip" Webb, a man who served as APA president from 2000 to 2003, pulled no punches while using most of one single-spaced page to attack voice stress-based challengers to the polygraph.

"I constantly receive horror stories where someone was unjustly accused or dropped from contention for a position of trust, based upon the results of a voice stress test," he explained. "Unfortunately, the greater danger is the stories we will never hear where someone else was deemed a better suspect because they failed these pseudo-scientific test."

After using much hyperbole-filled language critical of voice-stress technology, he implored APA members to take action.

"We have unsuspecting police chiefs and sheriffs out there trying to save money for the department and provide quality equipment for their officers and they are simply being fed a line of garbage," he continued. "Each of you must take it upon yourself to get involved and get the true information out to the decision makers so that bad decisions aren't made. We need to talk to city and county attorneys and city and county managers so that they don't approve the waste of public funds on these devices."

Before he finished, he explained that he had requested and received approval from the APA board to spend money to prepare and mail "accurate information out to every chief of police and sheriff and city and county manager in this country about the polygraph and voice stress."

On page three of the same newsletter, APA Board

Member T.V. O'Malley dedicated six paragraphs to the discussion of "Alternate Detection of Deception Technology Issues (ADDT)," explaining that they are "quite simply morally and ethically wrong" and "jeopardize the rights and freedoms and liberty of every American citizen."

After describing the alternate technologies as "Ouija Board science," he informed APA members about future efforts to combat ADDT.

"As you will see in an upcoming special edition of the Polygraph Journal, ADDT methodologies do not work and should never be relied on to formulate opinions of truth, deception, guilt, or innocence," he explained, closing the paragraph with a clear message, "There is no better mousetrap."

Months later, the special edition of the APA's quarterly newsletter, *Polygraph*, arrived in mailboxes around the country.

Among the 100-plus pages of the pseudo-scientific journal stuffed with advertisements touting all things polygraph, readers found a dozen articles containing details of studies in which non-polygraph technologies were declared flawed for a variety of reasons.

Atop the list of studies appearing in the publication was one[19] published in 2002 that produced the less-than-surprising conclusion, "As a practical consideration, the poor validity for the current voice stress technology should provide a caveat to agencies considering adding voice stress to their investigative toolboxes."

Who came up with those conclusions? Three deeply-entrenched polygraph loyalists: Donald J. Krapohl, Ph.D.; Andrew H. Ryan Jr., Ph.D.; and Kendall W. Shull.

A researcher at Polygraph Headquarters, Dr. Krapohl had already received no fewer than three APA awards and would, four years later, become president of the world's largest association of polygraph professionals.

Dr. Ryan was chief of research at Polygraph Headquarters and had been selected to serve as liaison between government polygraph officials and National Research Council (NRC) researchers as the latter group worked to produce the 2002 report, "THE POLYGRAPH AND LIE DETECTION,"[20] republished by the National Academy of Sciences (NAS) in 2003.

Shull was running his own business, Kendall Shull Investigations and Polygraph Services, in Knoxville, Tennessee, after retiring from his job as chief of the FBI's Polygraph Unit.

Before moving beyond this "scientific" study, it's worth pointing out that its conclusion section included a link to another voice stress-bashing website, http://voicestress.org. Not surprisingly, that website was registered[21] January 20, 2001, under the name of then-APA President Webb.

# CHAPTER FOUR:
# 'Global War on Terror'

Within hours of the attacks that left thousands of Americans dead and injured and exposed vulnerabilities in our nation's defenses, President George W. Bush tried to calm fears and assure Americans – including many who wanted to exact some form of retaliation against those they believed were responsible for the attacks -- that everything was under control September 11, 2001.

"America was targeted for attack because we're the brightest beacon for freedom and opportunity in the world," he told Americans during a nationally televised speech the night of the attacks. "And no one will keep that light from shining."

He used a more-ominous tone to end his remarks.

"The search is underway for those who are behind these evil acts," he said. "I've directed the full resources for our intelligence and law enforcement communities to find those responsible and bring them to justice. We will make no distinction between the terrorists who committed these acts and those who harbor them."

Two days later, President Bush spoke again -- this time before a joint session of Congress.

Among other things, he thanked lawmakers for "delivering $40 billion to rebuild our communities and meet the needs of our military."

It went without saying that our nation was about to enter a new era of warfare unlike any Americans had seen before. For nearly nine years, it would be referred to as the "Global War On Terror."

On October 7, 2001, at 12:30 p.m. Eastern Daylight Time, the United States and Great Britain began using air, land, and sea assets to launch bombs and cruise missiles against Taliban positions across Afghanistan. The first official GWOT campaign, Operation Enduring Freedom, had begun, and Americans were now fighting in unfamiliar territory -- in places with names like Bagram, Jalalabad, and Kandahar.

* * *

Three months into the war and thousands of miles from the rugged, mountainous terrain where Soviet forces had fought unsuccessfully against Afghan resistance forces (a.k.a., "Mujahideen") a quarter-century earlier, the first 20 of more than 700 detainees (a.k.a., "enemy combatants" or "prisoners of war") arrived at the U.S. Naval Station Guantanamo (a.k.a., "GITMO").

At the little-talked-about facility where the United States has maintained a military presence since 1903, the detainees would be subjected to a variety of interrogation methods employed by U.S. military and intelligence officials seeking information that might help the U.S.-led war effort succeed.

News reports about those interrogation methods -- both real and imagined -- would make the name of the U.S. outpost on the southeast tip of Cuba familiar to people worldwide.

One man with more than a passing interest in what detainees might reveal to interrogators was Army Major General Geoffrey D. Miller. Ten months after the first detainee arrived at GITMO, he assumed command of Joint Task Force Guantanamo (JTF-GTMO).

As head of the joint (a.k.a., "purple suit") organization comprised of people from a variety of military agencies, he was responsible for everything having to do with the detainees, including the arduous task of interrogating each of them.

Despite the seemingly urgent mission of learning as much as possible from the detainees, General Miller found it difficult during his first year on island to obtain polygraph support for his mission, according to "Charlie."

Not his real name, which I'm withholding for security reasons, Charlie served as operations officer (i.e., second in charge) of the DIA's Interrogation Control Element (ICE) at GITMO from early 2003 to mid-2004, longer than any officer preceding him in that post.

Well after his departure from Cuba, Charlie explained in a "To Whom It May Concern" letter, dated October 5, 2005, that polygraphers had repeatedly cited "numerous worldwide commitments" in their negative responses to General Miller's requests for assistance. In addition, he wrote, "We were not a priority." *NOTE: I was able to obtain a copy of Charlie's letter on the condition I not reveal his real name or the name of the person who provided me the copy. Though the author listed several individuals by name in his letter, I opted to remove most of those names due to concerns about their personal safety. Only the general's name remains due to the fact that his position as commander of Joint Task Force-Guantanamo received much publicity.*

Charlie went on to explain how polygraphers began to show interest -- but only after his proposal to move forward with CVSA® Proof of Principle (PoP) testing at GITMO received approval from the ICE chief, a colonel.

In addition, he wrote about some of the problems GITMO interrogators had experienced with the polygraph. His words revealed he did not appear to be constrained by the boundaries of official Army thinking as he shared details about his 16-month stay on island, which included being there "when the polygraph was first employed on a more permanent basis."

"We had to close a couple of our interrogation booths so that they could be dedicated to polygraphers and their equipment," Charlie wrote before adding a bit about what he knew about both polygraph and CVSA® from previous observation and training.

"The primary goal of any polygraph or CVSA examination is to facilitate voluntary admissions and confessions from the subject," he explained before noting, "Voluntary admissions and confessions are most likely to be truthful."

Charlie continued his letter by explaining that a conversation takes place during the pre-test phase to convince the subject "if he is deceptive in his answers, he will be found out" and "he must clear his mind of anything that may be bothering him that would cause a response to appear deceptive during the examination" in order to successfully "pass" the examination.

In other words, Charlie explained, "He must 'come clean' with the examiner."

"During the pretest phase, the examiner can also gather information and 'tailor' questions designed to gather additional information from the subject at the conclusion of the examination," Charlie wrote.

Deeper into his letter, Charlie highlighted several distinct advantages CVSA® has over the polygraph.

He explained that CVSA® technology is more portable, less intrusive (microphone as opposed to galvanic, heart, blood pressure, and breathing monitors) and requires less training on the part of the examiners.

Further, he wrote, the CVSA® test is easier to explain to the subject before it is administered, test results are easier to explain to the subject, and charts for both control questions and relevant questions can be shown and explained. That, in turn, makes post-test questioning much easier.

Charlie pointed out that there are no "inconclusive" test results with CVSA® and that examiners can identify the questions to which the subject's answers appeared to show deception -- an aspect that helps to focus additional questions and subsequent interrogations.

Conversely, Charlie noted that polygraphers would not identify the questions about which interrogation subjects appeared to be deceptive. Instead, they would only say the test showed "no deception indicated," "deception indicated" or "inconclusive."

Charlie used some pointed language to close his letter.

"My opinion based upon my observation is that CVSA is superior to the polygraph when used as a tool in the interrogation process. Consequently, I conclude that those who wish to remove CVSA from the 'interrogator's tool box' are more interested in protecting their turf than they are in gathering intelligence that protects the American people."

Beyond Charlie's letter, the content of an After Action Review (AAR) written by another senior interrogation official at GITMO -- a man I'll call "Hank" -- paints a clear picture of the

CVSA® PoP testing results. As was the case with Charlie's letter, I was able to obtain a copy of the AAR written by Hank from a confidential source promised anonymity.

Corroborating timelines and other details from Charlie's letter, Hank explained that CVSA® PoP testing began August 18, 2003, with seven GITMO interrogators being trained for six days in how to conduct exams using CVSA®. Equipment and training were provided by NITV.

Eight days after the training began, GITMO interrogators began using CVSA® as a tool to assist in targeting future interrogation efforts, he continued. Their efforts at the facility -- then home to more than 600 detainees from Afghanistan and Iraq as well as several other Middle Eastern and Southwest Asian countries -- continued for 30 days, through September 26, 2003.

Hank explained that it became obvious during the test period that CVSA® "would become an invaluable tool for focusing the efforts of intelligence collection."

By virtue of using CVSA®, he continued, "interrogations could be focused on areas where deception is indicated, versus wasting time and energy on avenues of exploitation that would have little to no value. The outcome of the 30 day test period has shown outstanding results, and has generated a high degree of interest and satisfaction among the intelligence community."

In the remainder of the document, Hank explained that the seven trained interrogators conducted 45 separate examinations on 33 different examinees. The examinations were conducted in English, Arabic, Pashtu, and Spanish on examinees -- all male -- who ranged in age from 17 to 65. Language was not a barrier.

Interestingly, Hank noted that, while the majority of the exams were conducted overtly, nine were conducted covertly (i.e., recorded for later analysis or having the computer located in an area not visible to examinee).

Six examinations were scored as "No Deception Indicated"; 38 as "Deception Indicated"; and one as "unable to be scored due to recording difficulties experienced with the recording media" -- a non-CVSA® technical glitch, Hank explained. When it became obvious that CVSA® PoP testing had yielded stellar results, GITMO officials stopped the testing halfway into the planned 60-day test period. They had seen enough.

Early the next year, NITV officials were contacted by DIA's chief interrogator on island -- a man I'll call "Ronald" -- who proposed the company enter into a two-year contract to provide the agency a subject-matter expert for the purpose of training additional interrogators at GITMO and providing other expertise as needed. A contract was signed and, by mid-2004, the company had one of its senior instructors working on the island.

During the next 12 months, according to NITV officials, CVSA® was used at GITMO more than 90 times and achieved a success rate -- defined as developing new, previously-unknown intelligence which was independently confirmed or confirmed existing information that otherwise could not be verified -- of 92 percent despite the fact most exams were conducted using interpreters.

That level of success stood in stark contrast to the "inconclusive" findings that had resulted from 20 percent of the polygraph exams administered previously at GITMO

# CHAPTER FIVE:
## 'Deck of Cards'

Less than a month after CVSA® PoP testing ended at GITMO, one man's reputation as one of the world's top CVSA® examiners landed him a 90-day assignment during which he put the technology to another test halfway around the world. The man -- whom I'll call "Ed" because revealing his real name could put him in danger -- spoke with me about his unique experience with CVSA®.

"In October of 2003, I went to Baghdad as a contractor for (the Defense Intelligence Agency)," Ed said. "During that time, I ran approximately 50 examinations."

Among those he examined were several individuals, collectively known as the "Deck of Cards," who had served in high positions within the Iraqi government before the April 2003 collapse of the Saddam Hussein regime.

"I did Tariq Aziz. I did the vice president of the country. I did Saddam's little brother," he said. "Every one of those people had been (polygraph) tested before I got there, and every (polygraph exam) was 'inconclusive.'"

Most of the high-value people in the dictator's inner circle had been educated in the United States and were familiar with countermeasures to defeat the polygraph, Ed explained.

"They knew all about it, so they weren't scared at all about the polygraph."

Things were altogether different when CVSA® entered the picture.

"I was able to convince them that this was the latest equipment from the United States of America, very few people know how to do this, and my government has sent me over here to see if you're withholding any information -- and, if you are, I'll know immediately.

"I was able to tell them immediately, and I was able to get a lot of good information from them."

In addition to the Deck of Cards, Ed said he also tested members of the Taliban and Al-Qaeda during the next eight years.

One of those sessions took place in a distant foreign country -- the name of which he could not share due to security reasons -- and involved testing a high-value terror suspect who, despite being interrogated for seven days prior to Ed's arrival, had revealed nothing.

"I tested him and, within five minutes after the examination, he started talking and, basically, gave (up) all kinds of stuff," Ed said.

CVSA® had clearly worked for Ed, who is also an expert polygraph examiner. While answering questions about why and how it worked, he outlined his belief that one of the biggest differences between CVSA® and the polygraph is that individuals can use several types of countermeasures to affect the polygraph.

"They can control their breathing," he explained. "Any muscle movement will affect the polygraph chart; and, certainly, if (suspects) have been schooled and they can do it at the right time, they can come up, at least, with an inconclusive chart where the examiner has a very difficult time making a decision.

"With the CVSA, there are virtually no countermeasures. There's really nothing (a person) can do that wouldn't be obvious to the examiner -- you know, raise and lower their voice, refuse to answer the control questions or just basically not answer.

"To me, it's a lot better instrument," Ed continued. "It's a lot more user-friendly, and I certainly have a lot more confidence using the CVSA as well as analyzing the charts. They're just so much easier to handle."

Two American government employees with whom Ed worked in Iraq praised his work in letters following his departure.

A strategic interrogator at the Joint Interrogation Debriefing Center, Iraqi Survey Group, in Baghdad, sent an undated letter to Ed's employer about his work.

"In mid December," the letter began, "Ed and I conducted an interrogation coupled with a Computerized Voice Stress Analyzer of a former high level Iraqi Regime member (hereinafter the source).

"During the preliminary questioning phase, which lasted two hours, the source was very calm and controlled as he continually provided misleading and evasive answers to all relevant questions, particularly those that incriminated him in crimes. I turned the interrogation over to Ed for his preparations for the CVSA of information just provided by the source and I left the room.

"The source had previously failed a CVSA with Ed and immediately his non-verbal communication observed on camera suggested that he was experiencing acute anxiety at the prospect of another test. The best example of this was when he had to use his stocking cap to mop his forehead of sweat several times, and this was just as Ed was going over the questions prior to the test. Ed then was able to get the source to admit to crucial information that he had denied and avoided in all previous interrogations.

"The source repeatedly said he did not like the machine and did not think that it worked," the letter continued. "I came back in the room and together we extracted as much of the crucial information as we could without postponing the test much more.

"Ed then conducted the test and the source showed stress in regards to a subject that took us all by surprise and will further implicate the source in crimes against humanity.

"I have worked this source for months without significant progress in getting him to admit guilt and provide candid responses. I fully ascribe the success of this interrogation to the CVSA's ability to be used quickly and simply in conjunction with the approaches of the interrogators. Moreover, the fact that the CVSA can be repeatedly used to teach the interrogation team about a particular source is unparalleled.

"This is a very powerful and easy to use tool," the strategic interrogator concluded. "It just doesn't get any better than that in a strategic interrogation environment like Ed and I have been working here in Iraq."

Another letter, dated January 12, 2004, was written by the noncommissioned officer in charge of the Iraq Survey Group's Mobile Collection Element and describes the letter writer's experience with Ed and CVSA®.

"From October 2003 to January 2004, Ed assisted the Iraq Survey Group using the Computer Voice Stress Analyzer (CVSA) system," the letter began. "He worked tirelessly under dangerous and austere conditions, assisting in source debriefings in the most dangerous sections of downtown

Baghdad. He also assisted in debriefings of High Value Detainees held by coalition forces, and conducted CVSA tests of coalition employees in sensitive positions.

"In assisting the mobile collection element downtown, Ed conducted CVSA testing on coalition sources to verify immediately actionable information. His efforts allowed my team members to assess reliability of information to be used in planning and conducting anti-insurgency operations. Because of the increased certainty Ed's tests lent to the information, coalition units could act with greater decisiveness and certainty.

"I have complete confidence in his judgment and competence in his field of work," the letter writer concluded. "I would work with Ed again without hesitation and would highly recommend his use to other United States Military entities."

Despite such high praise for his work, Ed made a point of telling me he considers both the polygraph and CVSA® to be tools and nothing more.

"Neither one of them is perfect," he said. "They both do the same job. One just goes about it differently than the other. That's really all there is to it.

"I certainly prefer the CVSA -- mainly because of the countermeasures issue and all that -- but, I mean, they're both tools. That's all they are.

"As much as I believe in the CVSA, just because somebody fails the test, I'm not gonna lock 'em up in prison for the rest of their life, but (the test results) will certainly give me an idea of how much more work I need to do to get the information."

# CHAPTER SIX:
# 'Truckloads of Bad Guys'

In addition to the conflicting reports from GITMO and Baghdad, I received detailed input from Army, Marine Corps, and Navy warfighters whose careers had taken them to many of the world's hotspots. Some of the best blow-by-blow accounts I received, however, surfaced during my interview with "Joe," a member of an Army Special Forces Group (SFG) trained in counterintelligence and as an interrogator.

While serving in countries like Afghanistan, Iraq, Kuwait, and Qatar, Joe used CVSA® to interrogate various types of people. Among those he questioned were third-country nationals (TCNs) seeking employment at U.S. bases, captured enemy combatants and others deemed to pose possible threats to U.S. and allied troops.

Regularly working 18-hour days during a five-year period beginning in 2004, Joe used CVSA® to conduct nearly 500 interrogations — more than any other individual in the U.S. military and nearly half of the total number of exams conducted by Army SFGs during that time period.

Following his retirement from the Army, Joe spoke with me about his firsthand experiences with CVSA® on the condition I not reveal his real name. After I agreed to his terms, he shared four true stories.

The first story Joe shared had to do with an old building in the Baghdad area to which Special Forces (SF) operators brought detainees upon returning from a mission. Known as

55

How did he determine the stories were true? CVSA?

"The Barn," it got its name, Joe said, by virtue of the fact it had several rooms that looked something like horse stalls.

Located in the same neighborhood as the facility housing the Iraqi Special Operations Forces (ISOF -- a.k.a., "Iraqi Commandos") -- and members of the U.S. Special Operations Forces from all branches of the military, The Barn operated like a police station in many ways, Joe said. It had a booking room, evidence room, holding cells and interview rooms, thanks largely to doors being added to the stalls to provide some degree of privacy when SF operators brought detainees to the facility.

Joe and his colleagues had to be very careful there, he said, because "as the lawyers got involved in this deal and the more time went on, it was more like trying to convict somebody in court than it was to pull a terrorist off the street, or a bad guy off the street."

Part of being "careful" involved providing medical treatment.

"The doc would check 'em out, (because) they got banged up a little bit whenever we came to get 'em," he continued. "They would address all (of) their wounds and stuff like that."

"We could hold 'em there up to a couple of days before we had to make a decision on whether to transfer to our detainee facility, go to (Camp) Cropper, release to the Iraqis, so forth and so on. There were about five different ways we could go with them from that area."

That was the first place where they used CVSA® to interview detainees, he said, adding that they often had "truckloads of bad guys" coming in there and only two counterintelligence or two human intelligence (HUMINT) agents there to handle the load.

"When you're trying to figure out how not to cut the bad guy loose and keep the good guy in custody, CVSA was an invaluable tool," Joe said, explaining that CVSA® enabled them to answer questions such as, "Do we have the right guy sitting in this cell?"

"We would get their initial statement when we brought them in," he said. "Then we would come back a day or two later with the CVSA and vet that story.

"We weren't determining guilt or innocence," he continued. "What we were determining was, 'Does this guy need any further work or warrant any further effort on our part to try and extract any intelligence from him?'"

Though he was involved in bringing detainees in from target sites, Joe noted that military intelligence people processed detainees through, got their initial stories and so forth.

"I didn't want to be involved with the processing of them, because I would run into them again later if they were to be developed into a source; then I would run them for further targeting.

"So I didn't want them to know who I was. I was just some dude with a mask that came to their house. They didn't have any clue who I was in case I had to meet them later in a different capacity."

Upon detecting my interest in his stories about happenings at The Barn, Joe made a point of clearing up some of the lies circulating in the press about mistreatment of detainees by U.S. forces.

"The very first thing that they get after they come in and they get their photos — and, of course, we make sure that they're absolutely clean for our own safety — (is) they go to their stalls, they're given water, the Iraqi soldiers feed 'em Iraqi food," he said. "They're able to be escorted to the bathroom, they're no longer blindfolded, the whole deal."

As for the rumors that inspection teams were not being allowed into the facility because detainees were being beaten there, Joe said The Barn wasn't inspected because it was a holding facility for further transfer and, as such, wasn't subject to inspection.

The reason they were successful at getting information from detainees wasn't because they tortured them, he explained, it was because they did the opposite as a condition for using CVSA® with success.

"I couldn't even put a number to the man-hours CVSA has saved me," Joe said. "There's no way to check or vet or verify any information in a country where every ID is fake, all the government systems are down, people who are enrolling in government systems aren't enrolling under true names in case (someone) ever digs up their old names — you know, they're trying to get a new start at life.

"There's just no way to check anything over there other than some type of truth-verification system."

On more than one occasion, Joe said, CVSA® played a direct role in saving American and Iraqi soldiers' lives.

On one such occasion, Joe used CVSA® to help identify an infiltrator.

"We were getting ready to hit a target," Joe said. "It was a time-sensitive target."

Joe explained that two Iraqi brothers were playing key roles in the operation. One was with Joe and his men, while the other was on target with the bad guys and reporting back as to their location, the exact time when a meeting was to take place and when the "good guys" could go in and snatch up some key players on the other side.

While they were waiting, Joe said, a call came in, advising them that the meeting was going to take place in one hour.

"Everybody scrambles, and the only people that knew, up until this briefing, that this was even on the target deck and that these sources existed, were Americans," Joe explained. "Once we briefed the target to the Iraqi leadership, they broke away and they went and briefed their guys."

From the time Joe's team was notified, briefed the Iraqi leadership and released them so they could brief their own guys about the mission, he said, 40 minutes had elapsed.

Then, another phone call came in from the brother working in the enemy camp, Joe said. His message was urgent: "Hey, man, they know you're coming! They're hauling ass right now! Somebody called 'em and told them!"

"So we lock everybody down that had knowledge to that point," he explained. "When we locked everybody down that had knowledge to that point, you've gotta remember, it's me and another guy that are getting ready to go and investigate this.

"So, we're sitting there, and they blow this," Joe said. "At this point, I go to find out who knows, and the pool of individuals who could possibly tip the target was 96 individuals."

Joe said they decided to lock down all 96 potential turncoats in the conference room at the theater. Working without sleep during the next 48 hours, they "CVSA'd" every one of them, asking if they had attended the briefing or made any unauthorized phone calls.

"At the end of that, we had three people that couldn't clear the charts," Joe said, "It was the lieutenant colonel, the sergeant major, and his driver.

The only reason the driver was snared, Joe said, was because of the rule that, once the target is called, nobody was supposed to have a cell phone.

"The colonel told the sergeant major to call the people on the target and let him know that we were coming," Joe explained. "The sergeant major told the driver to go get his phone and bring it to him. The driver didn't know what he was using it for.

"Basically, we took a 96-man suspect pool, narrowed it down to three individuals, and then confirmed... that the results of the CVSA were correct by breaking those guys in interrogation afterward."

Unfortunately, infiltrators were not Joe's only problem.

In a another story, Joe outlined how CVSA® proved its value after U.S. forces began suspecting an ammunition theft ring was operating at the school where members of the Iraqi Special Operations Forces trained to become operators as members of the 36th Commandos.

Suspicions surfaced after Americans recovered some of their own ammunition at target sites (i.e., locations where they had engaged the enemy), Joe said. That's when investigators began looking at the school's 24 Iraqi instructors.

"I went down there, and I brought every instructor in, and we CVSA'd them," Joe said. "One-hundred percent accurate, I had the ringleader and all eight guys that were stealing ammunition nailed from the first interview.

"That focused my efforts down to those nine individuals and let the other dudes go that didn't have anything to do with it, didn't know what was going on.

"After the CVSA results, we went down and searched their barracks and, in all of their rooms, we found ammunition — stowed up in the ceilings, in their drawers, wrapped up in socks. All kinds of stuff. I mean, they had ammo everywhere in those nine rooms.

"We searched all the other rooms, and we had one guy that had some ammunition, but we think he kept it for personal use, that he was just trying to have some extra ammo to take to the house. He wasn't selling it and didn't know that those guys were."

During the investigation, Joe learned exactly how nine of the school's 24 Iraqi instructors had been stealing ammunition from the school.

"They would have each one of the candidates each day that were coming through the course hand them one stripper clip of ammunition — of 5.56 or a half a box of 9mm or some .762 or whatever it was," he said, adding that the instructors then took the ammunition — and its packaging which nobody tracked — back to their rooms for repackaging.

The subordinate instructors, Joe explained, sold their ammo for 50 percent value to the head instructor, and the head guy repackaged it and sold it for full value on the black market. Then they all received a return on their money.

Less glamorous but equally critical, according to Joe, was the use of CVSA® in screening TCNs applying for employment on U.S. military installations. In a fourth and final story, Joe told me how his initial use of CVSA® for that purpose took place in Qatar and Kuwait.

"We were able to pick up the numbers screened by over 300 percent in a day by using the CVSA," he explained, "(because) we actually had viable information that we could look at and check as to whether or not they were telling the truth."

When screening people outside of the United States, he explained that SF operators don't have access to National Crime Information Center and Department of Motor Vehicle records or to school and college records, resulting in "really no way to check these guys out."

What did SF operators do prior to having CVSA® when it came to screening TCNs who, by definition, are already out of their countries of origin (i.e., Nepal, Philippines, Thailand, etc.)? Joe described what would happen during the pre-CVSA® era if he thought a guy was a bad guy and took time to write an inquiry containing questions — "Does this guy have any criminal record? Any criminal history?" — and send it to their country's embassy in Iraq.

"This guy's already out of (his) country, working somewhere else, and sending all the money he makes back to his country, to improve their economy," he said. "Is their embassy actually going to send us a thing saying, 'Yeah, he's a criminal; send him back'? I'm thinking, 'No.'

"We never got a hit the entire time when we were sending these things out, and I was thinking, 'This is ridiculous!'" Joe said.

"They are not going to tell us that this guy is skimping on his child support or he used to be a thief or whatever the deal is. They've already got him out of the country, and he's sending every dollar he makes back to his family and improving the economy of his own country. Why in the hell would they tell us that so we could send him back?"

Asked how many times he sent them out?

"Thousands," Joe said. "My TCN list when I was in Kuwait was over 15,000 TCNs working on the nine base camps in Kuwait.

"We screened five days a week from 8 o'clock in the morning to 5 o'clock in the afternoon," he added, explaining that a total of four agents were responsible for screenings at nine base camps."

During the year he was there, Joe said, he and his colleagues didn't even finish screening the employees who worked in retail stores and restaurants operated by the Army and Air Force Exchange Service (AAFES), not to mention the security guys, the septic truck drivers, just to name a few.

Suspecting TCNs were "robbing us blind" at U.S. bases in the region, Joe said he set up a five-day search at the exit to Camp Arab John in Kuwait and was able to recover more than $1.2 million worth of stolen property — "drugs, alcohol and all kinds of stuff."

Prior to that, he said, commanders were always asking him, "Who screened this guy?" after someone was caught stealing.

Joe said he would reply, saying, "Hey look, man, you're telling me to screen the guy, then you don't give me any way to check the information that he tells me, but then you want me to sign off, sayin' he's an okay guy and let him come to work on the base. You've gotta give me a tool to help me with this."

CVSA® became that tool — the "perfect match," he added.

"If they don't clear the chart, then we continue to interview and, if we can't get them through the process of a little longer interview and we can't get 'em to clear the chart, then we just deny them employment. It's just that easy, because there's a question of doubt there."

Incredibly, much of Joe's use of CVSA® took place after top government officials had declared the polygraph DoD's only approved credibility assessment technology. Even after those occasions, which will be explained in detail later in this book, Joe continued using CVSA® in the field.

Why? Because of the answer he received after going to his commander and asking the question, "You want me to stop?"

"Hell no, don't stop!" his commander replied. "You're just not using it anymore, right?"

Joe said his commanders wanted him to continue using CVSA® for one primary reason: They knew it was far superior to PCASS when it came to dealing with people who might pose threats to U.S. interests. And guys like Joe knew how to keep things like CVSA® "off the books."

In places like Iraq, where CVSA® worked so effectively, Joe said, he could tell an interview subject, "Hey, you're gonna be here for a really long time and convicted as a terrorist if I find out you're lying to me." Conversely, he could say, "You're gonna go home tomorrow if you clear this chart."

In other words, jeopardy was clearly present.

In stark contrast to the official message coming from headquarters, Joe told me SF operators would "rather go back to the stubby pencil and taking an educated guess" than use PCASS in place of CVSA®.

One of the major flaws in the technology that cause Joe and others to discount PCASS can be found in polygraph training, Joe said, that involves mock scenarios where subjects are given roles to play prior to undergoing a polygraph exam.

"If you can trick yourself into thinking you're a bomber," Joe said, referring to a 2006 PCASS study[22] conducted at Fort Jackson, "then why can't you trick yourself into thinking you're not and trick that machine?"

Joe added that he thinks rank-and-file polygraphers would embrace CVSA® if given the opportunity.

"If you take PCASS operators and CVSA operators, cross-train 'em and, at the end of that, give 'em some time to work with the equipment in the field, I would say 95 to 96 percent of them guys — because, you know, some people just don't like change if they were PCASS guys first — will tell you that the CVSA is a much better piece of equipment."

I asked Joe what he would say if given the chance to speak to our nation's leaders in Washington about the prohibition on the CVSA® use by U.S. troops.

"I would testify in front of Congress that this piece of equipment is essential for (HUMINT) personnel on the ground in Iraq and Afghanistan," he said. "If they want to save lives, they've got to put this piece of equipment back into that theater. Every unit should have this equipment."

At the time of our interview, Joe could not -- or, perhaps, would not -- tell me with certainty whether or not SF operators in the field were still bucking authority by using CVSA®, but he did have a message for those who remain opposed to CVSA®.

"Anybody looking out for the welfare of the Soldier and really looking at this open-minded (would) see that the CVSA is the best tool for the job," he said, noting later that someone in Army leadership was more willing to rely upon laboratory studies commissioned by officials and agencies with vested interests in the polygraph instead of trusting operational research like that in which Joe had been engaged almost daily.

# CHAPTER SEVEN:
# 'Hell of a Tool'

In addition to proving itself capable overseas, CVSA® made a name for itself as a reliable tool for use by investigators at law enforcement agencies across the United States.

Every one of the U.S. law enforcement officers with whom I spoke about CVSA® said he considers the technology a vital tool in his crime-fighting toolkit. At the same time, however, each insisted it is *only* a tool -- not an end-all solution -- for eliciting confessions and/or solving crimes. Finally, each told me during 2012 interviews that his goal when using CVSA® is to ensure innocent people are set free and guilty people are not.

In Columbus, Ohio, Mike DeFrancisco is a fire/arson investigator with more than 20 years of law enforcement experience in the city. A graduate of the city's police academy, he is assigned to the city's fire department.

"We generally use it to rule people in and out as suspects," said DeFrancisco, who, at the time of my interview, had been using CVSA® for five years.

One case he described as a good example of the effectiveness of CVSA® took place during the summer of 2007 and involved 42-year-old arson suspect Christopher Daniel Bagley.

As a result of CVSA® exams on Bagley and on his daughter, who Bagley had accused of being involved in setting fires, DeFrancisco was able to rule out the daughter as the perpetrator and determine Bagley was the serial arsonist who had set several fires within a three-week period at a vacant house two doors down from his own home.

Notably, DeFrancisco added, Bagley had been through a polygraph before, but passed. He had also been subjected to a CVSA® exam as part of an unrelated case and showed deception.

"It's a hell of a tool, and we have great results with it," he said.

As for his pre-CVSA® experience, DeFrancisco said he and his colleagues used polygraph before, but recognized its drawbacks.

"It seemed like we were always coming up with a lot of inconclusives," he said, and that resulted in guys being reluctant to use it.

In addition to logging a confession/plea bargain rate around 90 percent when examining suspects, DeFrancisco said his department's arrest rates are up at least 20 percent since switching from polygraph to CVSA® -- a number he said was substantially higher than the national average.

Recently retired, Lieutenant David Wyllie was a criminal investigator in Florida who headed up the Citrus County Sheriff's Office Special Victims Unit.

In addition to the aforementioned caveats, he made two more things clear to me at the outset of my interview with him: (1) He was not loyal to polygraph or CVSA®; and (2) His equipment choices are always made to enhance his ability to solve crimes.

Without question, the most high-profile investigation in which Lieutenant Wyllie's been involved during more than 30 years in law enforcement was the Jessica Lunsford murder case that captivated the nation's attention in 2005.

In that case, the lieutenant said, a CVSA® exam of the girl's father, Mark Lunsford, cleared him while polygraph exams conducted by the Florida Department of Law Enforcement and the FBI yielded conflicting results -- one "deceptive" and the other "inconclusive."

In the end, however, the results of a CVSA® exam of Mark Lunsford proved accurate after John Evander Couey, a 46-year-old convicted sex offender, confessed to abducting the nine-year-old girl from her grandparents' Homosassa, Florida, home in the middle of the night February 23, 2005, and then burying her alive.

As administrator of the State of Arkansas Sex Offender Screening and Risk Assessment Program, Sheri Flynn and her three examiner colleagues at the Arkansas Department of Corrections Administrative Complex in Pine Bluff had used CVSA® for more than two years at the time of our interview. Today, they continue to conduct exams of convicted sex offenders, most of whom are no longer behind bars.

Not only does having internal CVSA® examiners save time, Flynn said, but it's also much less costly than contracting out polygraph services.

Emphasizing that her words represent her personal opinion and not an official agency view, Flynn explained one of the reasons she wanted her people trained in conducting CVSA® exams.

"When an offender is faced with (a CVSA) exam on the day of the interview, they are more willing, often times, to give up other victims," she said.

"Our assessment is like a puzzle. There are many different pieces of it," she said, before listing historical data, police records and other pieces as types of data they consider. "The CVSA is just one piece of that puzzle. There is not a single decision that's made strictly based on passing or failing, deceptive or no deception indicated."

If an offender has a history of unsubstantiated child maltreatment reports or substantiated (reports) but no convictions and they're being deceptive, Flynn said that becomes a big piece of the puzzle as well.

Regardless of the outcome of a CVSA® exam, Flynn said she is most interested in the pre- and post-test admissions offenders make and in how those offenders gained access to their victims so that future crimes might be prevented.

After reflecting on my communications with officials at GITMO, as well as with Ben, Joe and members of the U.S. law enforcement community, I remain shocked that CVSA® is not being used to vet uniform-wearing Afghans and TCNs in Afghanistan.

Heck, it's even being used in Mexico.

# CHAPTER EIGHT:
## 'Commander Simon'

Even after being tested and "passing" polygraph tests, many corrupt Mexican police officers and other public officials remain involved in criminal activities, says one man involved in fighting crime south of the U.S.-Mexican border.

Despite the fact that officials serving on Mexico's National Public Safety Council have conceded it would be physically impossible to administer polygraph tests to all of the country's 700,000 active-duty police officers, the same man believes conducting polygraph tests on every Mexican law enforcement official will do little to reduce the country's rampant corruption (i.e., kidnappings, extortions, murders, and other criminal activities).

As evidence, the man points to an incident that took place in the Guadalajara suburb of Morelos in the state of Jalisco made headlines around the world in mid-June 2012.

A video[23] that captured the incident and went viral soon after being published on the video-sharing site, YouTube®, begins by showing a large convoy of municipal police patrol units, commanded by a night-shift operations supervisor, arriving at a hotel. Several heavily-armed policemen are shown entering the hotel where they ask for the room numbers of three guests.

A short time later, the policemen can be seen marching out of the hotel with three men wearing only their underwear.

Hours after that, according to an Associated Press report[24], the men were found asphyxiated and beaten to death.

Today, according to same source, the public safety director and all police commanders who were involved in that incident are in jail.

Who is this man, my source of so much knowledge about crime in Mexico? He is, perhaps, the most-unique individual with whom I spoke while conducting research for this book.

A 50-something native of Caracas, Venezuela, this tall, dark-haired man goes by the name, "Commander Simon." For reasons that will become clear as you read further, he cannot reveal his true identity.

In April 2012, after I agreed to keep his name secret, he granted me access as the first investigative journalist ever to interview him and learn about his secretive world.

Commander Simon operates from an undisclosed location inside the United States and employs CVSA® -- instead of polygraph -- as a tool to fight organized crime in Mexico. Unlike most of CVSA® users, however, he has used the technology in covert fashion and in tandem with effective undercover tactics to singlehandedly put a sizable dent in the bottom lines of several Mexican drug and kidnapping cartels. As a result of his success, leaders of those cartels would like to see him dead.

Since 1998, Commander Simon has been extremely successful in helping Mexican governors deal with a never-ending stream of kidnapping cases, most of which require victims' family members or employers to pay seven-figure ransoms in exchange for the safe return of their loved ones or employees.

Bob McCarty

"The bad guys, they used public phones to make phone calls to their victims' family members to negotiate ransoms, so, in those days, I had a lot of (business)," Commander Simon explained. "My service was very useful, because I had good relations with all of the telecommunications companies in Mexico through my friends in Mexico City."

In the beginning, while serving as director of anti-kidnapping teams in Chihuahua state, those "good relations" made it possible for him to have access to a database containing the numbers and locations of every single public phone in the city of Ciudad Juarez and state of Chihuahua. Later, he was able to add numbers and locations in other states.

"Every time I had a phone call, I knew how to find out where the phone call was coming from -- and the police liked it!"

Commander Simon's use of analog technology, combined with old-fashioned investigation and intelligence-gathering skills, enabled him to help Mexican law enforcement agencies locate kidnappers so that they could be captured.

After suspected kidnappers were taken into custody, however, things often went bad for them as Mexican police officials used interrogation techniques that occasionally resulted in their suspects meeting untimely deaths.

Hoping to find a way to avoid such nasty interrogations, Commander Simon began looking for an alternative interrogation technology in 2000.

After first considering the polygraph, he said he soon concluded that he was wasting his time. After all, that technology was untenable as it would require him to bring in a suspected kidnapper and connect him to a number of wires and sensors. Soon, his attention was drawn to CVSA®.

Commander Simon explained what he needed to NITV officials. In turn, they described how their product, CVSA®, used a microphone, a laptop computer and a sophisticated software program to detect real-world stress -- or the absence thereof.

"I found out thru my expertise in time that, in 90 percent of the (kidnapping) cases, somebody that is known to the family members is the person sending information to the kidnapping gangs of who, how, where and how much," he explained. "It could be a family member, a servant, a driver, a secretary -- it could be anybody.

"It could actually be the neighbor," he continued. "So I said, 'How am I going to put a microphone on these guys? It's impossible.' So we have to do an undercover job."

Commander Simon went on to explain that NITV staffers responded favorably when he told them he needed to be able to covertly record conversations over the phone and then analyze the results.

"Then, I said, 'Wow! Now we have something good! Let me do some research and find out if it works.'"

Until that time, Commander Simon said, he was "recording everything. Phone conversations. Phone negotiations. Everything was recorded. More recordings than anybody else in the industry."

After completing basic CVSA® examiner training in January 2002 and learning how to conduct covert examinations, he used CVSA® for the first time on a case that had begun a few months earlier and would be remembered as one of his most difficult crisis-negotiation cases ever. Commander Simon shared an account of that case with me.

\* \* \*

After finishing breakfast one morning, he explained, 11-year-old Rodolfo Rochin Jr. and his younger brother carried backpacks as they walked down the stairs from the kitchen into the attached garage of their family's three-story home in Culiacan, a city in the northwestern state of Sinaloa, Mexico. There, they expected to climb into the family's minivan and have their father drive them to school. Such was their routine, Monday to Friday. Everything changed, however, when they found two masked men armed with high-caliber weapons waiting for them in the garage.

The men placed gags in the mouths of the two boys and their father before sealing their mouths with duct tape. Next, they covered Rodolfo Jr.'s head with a paper bag and told Rodolfo Sr. they would kill his son if their demands were not met. Finally, they took the boy away at gunpoint on the floor of his father's vehicle.

The kidnappers drove quickly through the streets of Culiacan to a nearby location where they switched vehicles, climbing into another waiting car.

When news of Rodolfo Jr.'s kidnapping reached officials in the capitol of the Mexican state of Sinaloa, Governor Juan Millan Lizarraga asked Commander Simon to handle the case.

In addition to the kidnappers, Commander Simon faced another obstacle -- the boy's father did not want to involve the police in the matter and, instead, wanted to simply comply with the kidnappers' demands and not listen to anyone else.

In short, the father felt intimidated and was overwhelmed by the demands of the kidnappers. As a result, Commander Simon's job was made more difficult.

During several telephone conversations over a period of a few days, Commander Simon was finally able to convince the father to allow him into the family home -- but only as an observer. He was transported to the Rochin home in the trunk of a car driven by one of the family members and, upon arrival, was met in the garage by the father, a man still suffering from the psychological trauma of having been kidnapped, himself, in similar fashion at age 16.

Equipped with his negotiating tools and enough clothes for a week, Commander Simon was prepared to remain inside the Rochin home until Rodolfo Jr. was returned safely.

Aided by the kidnapped boy's mother, Irais, Commander Simon gradually won the father's trust, and the father began accepting his advice regarding negotiations with the kidnappers. After a few days, the father fully placed the negotiations in the hands of his guest.

Numerous phone calls came in from the kidnappers during the first few days and voice samples were collected. Commander Simon studied the toll records of those calls and, with the help of members of the local police department's anti-kidnapping squad, he was able to trace the calls to their points of origin.

Fifteen days after the ordeal had begun, Francisco Franco Javier Murillo was arrested by Sinaloa State police at a public telephone in the small town of Navolato, 35 minutes west of Culiacan.

Initially, the suspect was interrogated by police investigators who used what Commander Simon described as "medieval" techniques that produced little in the way of useful results. Then Commander Simon conducted a CVSA® exam without the suspect's knowledge.

During the exam, officials learned the suspect's wife was the director of a children's school and that his uncle was a member of the state senate. Commander Simon seized on the latter fact as he conducted his covert CVSA® exam.

Using a structured interview format, Commander Simon began by asking a dozen questions, many of which were non-threatening questions (i.e., name, place of birth, place of residence, etc.). It was the suspect's answers to five of the questions, however, that paid off.

Murillo showed high stress when he responded to the question, "Do you know who kidnapped Rodolfo Jr?"

He did the same in response to the question, "Did you call from a pay phone to the Rochin's house?"

Asked if he had called from the same pay phone to the safe house, his negative reply was accompanied by high stress.

Finally, when he was asked two more probing questions -- "Do you know where Rodolfo Jr. is?" and "Did you kidnap Rodolfo Jr.?" -- he showed a great deal of stress.

During the post-exam interview, Commander Simon confronted Murillo with the results of the CVSA® exam, and the man confessed that he was involved in the kidnapping.

Based upon the results of the CVSA® and other data collected during the investigation, authorities were able to locate the house where they believed Rodolfo Jr. was being held. The boy's parents, however, refused to authorize a rescue by means of force, fearing he might be harmed.

Less than 24 hours later, the investigators received a phone call from another kidnapper who demanded that Rodolfo Jr.'s father meet their ransom demand of 200,000 U.S. Dollars (USD). In response, the father told the kidnapper they were only able to raise 240,000 pesos -- approximately 25,000 USD at the time. They agreed to accept that amount.

The kidnappers instructed the father to bring the money and drop it at a marked location along a highway in Culiacan.

When Commander Simon saw that kidnappers on the other side of the highway were watching the movements of law enforcement officials, he feared Rodolfo Jr. was in the kidnappers' car and ordered his commanders not to intercept.

The money drop took place, and Rodolfo Jr. was released on a downtown street. Soon after, he went to a local business and called his home. His grandfather answered the phone, learned of the boy's location and drove to pick him up.

Understandably, the first few hours after the recovery were full of joy, congratulations and tears. But other business took place as well.

For approximately one hour, Commander Simon debriefed Rodolfo Jr. away from members of his family -- including his father.

During that time, the boy drew a sketch of the safe house and described the home's layout and objects inside the house. He recalled smells coming in through the windows. And he remembered the sounds produced by children playing in the afternoon.

Though Commander Simon had made a preliminary identification of the safe house based upon already-collected technical intelligence, including toll records, a positive ID of the house had to be made.

Commander Simon asked the father and his son to accompany him and a group of police officers to the suspected safe house to which Murillo had made the phone call before being captured.

Upon arrival there, Rodolfo Sr. said, "This house belongs to a cousin who worked with us at my father's factory until a few months ago."

In front of the house was the kidnapping vehicle, complete with the blanket -- still in the same position on the floor where it had been two weeks earlier when kidnappers had used to cover up the boy as they drove through the streets of Culiacan.

When Commander Simon and his colleagues went inside the house, they found Guadalupe Felix Perez, the cousin and owner of the house who had been mentioned by the kidnapped boy's father. Perez, a man in his mid-20s, was interrogated on the spot and confessed immediately.

Solidifying their case, they found the house matched the sketch of the house provided by Rodolfo Jr. during the debriefing. In addition, they found other incriminating items: a .357 magnum revolver, a .45-caliber pistol, two masks, and a roll of duct tape.

Upon conclusion of the case, two kidnappers were arrested and convicted and began serving 28-year prison sentences.

\* \* \*

Based on the Rochin case, Commander Simon made it his policy to conduct covert CVSA® exams of all family members and close associates of kidnapping victims' families. He considers CVSA® "an invaluable investigative tool" in his work.

"Since those days, I have been using CVSA® in every single kidnapping case that I've had," Commander Simon said.

As was the case with the Rochin family, the process usually involves early-stage interaction with family members and others close to the family.

"What I do, basically, is generate a fluid conversation with the family members, introduce myself, etc.," he explained, "then I say, 'Please allow me to make a phone call once I get acquainted with the case so I can talk to you more in depth about what happened, what you have heard, what you have seen -- something that will lead me to help the family, to solve the case.

"My modus operandi, usually what I do, is I get inside the family member's house," he continued. "Sometimes, I stay inside the family's house. Then I get acquainted with the negotiator."

The negotiator, in most cases, is someone Commander Simon trains to deal over the phone with the bad guys. Often, it's the father, the mother or the brother of the victim.

"At the same time, I'm recording everything," he continued. "I'm recording all of the conversations between the bad guys and the family members. Also, that's how I get all of the information about all of the family members -- nephews, compadres, neighbors -- and then I collect all of their phone numbers and where they live."

After collecting that information, he said he tells each family member something like this: "Well, tomorrow, I'll call you because I would like to talk with you over the phone just for you to tell me more about what you have heard and seen."

The following day, he said, he calls every family member, beginning each call with friendly conversation that leads -- unbeknownst to the person on the receiving end of the call -- to him conducting an interview similar to the one he did in the Rochin case.

Commander Simon explained that his interview subjects never realize they're undergoing a CVSA® examination, because he never asks what he calls "control" questions -- that is, questions asked with the intention of getting someone to lie.

Instead, he asks each person to answer only questions relevant to the kidnapping case -- such as "Are you the family member?" and "Are you the brother?" -- based upon their previous conversations.

"So when I ask (a person) if there's anybody involved in this kidnapping case that he might know and he says, 'No,' and I see high stress level, then I have a suspect inside the family members. Ninety-percent of the time, we can say it's successful."

Commander Simon's success with CVSA® led to him working directly for the governors of Chihuahua, Sinaloa and Jalisco states in separate multi-year stints. Today, however, he finds himself working in a slightly-different capacity as an advisor with contracts signed directly between his U.S.-based company and each kidnapping victim's family or employer, depending upon the nature of the case.

"I record the negotiations between the bad guy and the lead negotiator from the family," he explained. "Plus, I take the voice print -- and I have my own voice print database -- and I help the police department."

When the police capture a suspect, he explained, their forensic department's experts can use that suspect's voice print to see if they can find a match with any voice prints collected during other kidnapping investigations.

"That's one of the ways to find out that the suspect the police have already captured is a good lead, because (of) the voice print match," he said.

"Then, if the police department would like for me to continue helping them, I might get on the phone and talk to the guy. Then, during the interview, what I do is I find out all the information that he is going to provide me about the case -- if he's involved, if he knows where the (kidnapping victim) is located, etc."

By reviewing the CVSA® charts produced during the phone call, Commander Simon said he can tell at what point the suspect is showing high levels of stress, often indicative of lying.

"Then, at the end of my interview, I talk to the chief investigator of the police department, and I say, 'You know what, through my research, I have found that the guy you have sitting in front of you, he's the guy, he participated. He was the main negotiator.'"

In addition to helping police pinpoint a kidnapper(s), Commander Simon said he often helps them determine the location of a kidnapping victim based on the suspect's answers to a set of four questions about the part of the city in which the kidnapping victim is being held -- "Is he in the north? Yes or no?" and "Is he in the south? Yes or no?" and so on.

"By the end, I can tell the police department, 'You know, the guy is showing a high level of stress on question number three, indicating the (kidnapping victim) is on the east side of the city or could be on the east side of the city.'"

"That's real good advice for the police department. They can concentrate all their forces on one sector of the city..." instead of wasting a lot of time, money, and other resources in other areas.

Though his role has changed slightly, his belief in the technology has only grown stronger.

"For me, the CVSA has been the most successful tool in finding (a person) in the first perimeter of the family members who is (working) with the kidnapping gang," Commander Simon said. "The CVSA has been an excellent tool to find out who is involved in an undercover way -- through the phones and using my recorder."

Asked whether he has encountered any legal hurdles related to his recording of phone conversation, he said he has not, in part, because of the way he facilitates such conversations.

"I always use the following statement: 'Would you please allow me to record our conversation due to the fact that so many (there are) so many points, that I will have to do my report, that it will be easier for me to go over the report.'"

Commander Simon went on to explain why that statement works so well.

"I am not interrogating a suspect," he said. "I'm just having an interview with a family member (who) I'm asking for him to help me to understand how the situation happened... a family member of a kidnapping victim who might help me understand the philosophy of the town and how (the people there) work...."

"I play very naive," he continued, explaining that he uses a variety of phrases -- "I don't know," "I'm trying to find out," and "Perhaps you might be able to help me."

"I like for the guys to talk from their hearts and say, 'Well, you know, last year, blah blah blah blah, I know that the bad guys were there and that the chief of police was involved blah blah blah...'" he explained.

"I get more information playing the naive guy that wants to help the family."

Commander Simon explained that, near the end of an interview, he'll say, "Let me just go over my notes and let me ask you something... if you can just give me three more minutes..." before asking a few baseline "yes" or "no" questions, such as "Is your name such-and-such?" and "Do you live in such-and-such town?"

Fully aware that a corrupt police department can become his worst enemy in solving a kidnapping case, he also asks questions about corruption in the local political environment.

"If I learn that, in that town, the police department is involved in the kidnappings," he said, "I'm the first one that's going to get killed."

So he asks some important questions.

"Do you know if the police department might have a police officer involved?"

"What do you think about the police officers in your neighborhood?"

"Are they involved with kidnapping gangs?"

Knowing the answers to those questions literally helps him stay alive.

"Undercover interviews are more productive than the manual way of interviewing bad guys in Mexico, because (the police) don't get nothing," Commander Simon said. "Sometimes, they might kill the guy while trying to get the truth. For me, it's easy to get the truth by only having a conversation with the guy over the phone."

Since 1998, Commander Simon said he has handled approximately 300 kidnapping cases that have resulted in almost 450 "bad guys" being sent to prison, usually for 28 years each per Mexican law.

# CHAPTER NINE:
## 'The Cambone Memo'

Based largely on results like those highlighted in the previous two chapters, CVSA® began attracting attention from people on both sides of the turf war. One of those people was Stephen A. Cambone.

Not only did Cambone fit Green Beret Joe's description of a bureaucrat more willing to rely upon lab studies than operational research, but he was, according to a report[25] by Jeffrey St. Clair, a man "so hated and feared inside the Pentagon that one general told the *Army Times*: 'If I had one round left in my revolver, I'd take out Stephen Cambone.'"

Cambone had been appointed by Secretary of Defense Donald Rumsfeld in March 2003 to serve as the nation's first USDI.

Though I had no way of knowing whether Cambone was, indeed, "so hated and feared," my research yielded evidence that he seemed to keep himself apprised of CVSA® successes at GITMO and the threat the voice-stress technology poses to polygraph loyalists.

Barely halfway through the first year of NITV's two-year contract at GITMO, Cambone issued an "Interim Department of Defense Policy for 'Truth' Credibility Assessment," a document I hereafter refer to as "The Cambone Memo."

Dated June 8, 2004, and addressed to the Secretaries and Inspectors General of the military departments as well as the Directors of defense agencies and DoD field activities, The Cambone Memo contained clear guidance.

"Several of your organizations have asked about the technologies that are authorized in the Department of Defense (DoD) for detecting truthfulness or deception," Cambone wrote. "The polygraph is the only DoD credibility assessment instrument approved for use to determine 'statement veracity.' This policy is contained in DoD Directive 5210.48. That document is being revised and will include additional guidance on this subject.

"My staff will expand and accelerate research for improved means of credibility assessment, including technologies beyond that of polygraph," he continued. "However, until the accuracy of such technologies is supported by validated independent research, field vetting and lessons learned, the polygraph will remain the sole instrument for eliciting statement veracity.

"Users of 'truth' Credibility Assessment instrumentation (other than polygraph) already fielded or employed shall by July 30, 2004, provide the Counterintelligence Field Activity with a written assessment reflecting instrument type and numbers, how such instruments were used, overall utility, validating factors, lessons learned, limitations, and depictions of 'success' or 'failure' irrespective of circumstance or context. This data will assist in the validation and approval of future technology."

Perhaps due to the fact Cambone was a new person in a new position, his memo didn't deliver the desired effect. Interrogators were still using CVSA® at GITMO. As a result, he was forced to send a team to the detention facility -- ostensibly to "assess" the situation on island -- less than five months after issuing the memo.

Dr. John Capps, a senior official at the Counterintelligence Field Activity (CIFA), then the parent organization of Polygraph Headquarters, headed the team sent to the island. Coincidentally (or not), Dr. Capps is also the brother of Michael H. Capps, former director at Polygraph Headquarters and former APA president.

Also on the team were three other gentlemen: Dr. Ryan, a polygraph loyalist described earlier in this book; John C. Brown, Ph.D.; and Donnie Dutton. Each brought unique contributions to the effort.

Dr. Brown brought polygraph-related crisis management experience to the team. It was during his watch as director of the Los Alamos National Laboratory in 1998 that Wen Ho Lee, one of Brown's computer scientists at the New Mexico facility, found himself facing 59 charges -- 58 of which were later dropped -- after the FBI alleged he had failed a polygraph.[26]

Rounding out the team was Dutton, a Polygraph Headquarters staffer who would go on to serve as APA president during the 2007-2008 term.

Following the team's visit to GITMO October 18-21, 2004, several events took place: Ronald, the DIA's chief interrogator at GITMO, was reassigned to DIA Headquarters in Virginia; DIA's contract with NITV was canceled; NITV's expert was ordered to leave the island; and the use of CVSA® at GITMO ended.

At the same time Cambone seemed intent on eliminating CVSA®, U.S. Special Operations Command (SOCOM) leaders found themselves wondering if they had a legitimate new tool on their hands. They had, after all, seen CVSA® exceed expectations as a tool for interrogating GITMO detainees, members of the Deck of Cards, and others.

To answer their question, they asked NITV officials to conduct a briefing about CVSA® in August 2004. Impressed by what they learned during the briefing, they followed up by asking NITV officials to develop a smaller, handheld version of their technology that would take advantage of an automatic-scoring algorithm that was under development at NITV. The resulting technology, dubbed the "Field Interrogation Support Tool (FIST)," earned NITV a contract worth almost $700,000 via the extremely-competitive Defense Acquisition Challenge Program (DACP).

If all went as planned, DACP funds would be allocated in January 2005, and the project would launch soon after. Unfortunately, things did not go as planned.

In early 2005, according to a well-placed source, SOCOM officials happened upon information that led them to suspect Cambone might cancel the FIST project. In response, they commissioned an independent survey of CVSA® examiners in U.S. law enforcement to determine the validity of the technology which, at the time, was being used by more than 1,400 state and local agencies.

That spring, representatives of law enforcement agencies in eight states were surveyed by an independent research team led by Dr. Gary Gallagher. The survey[27] revealed that seven years was the average length of time agencies had used CVSA® and that most had begun in 1998.

Ranging in rank from sergeant to major and boasting an average of 23 years of experience, 80 percent of survey respondents had been trained as CVSA® examiners and had an average of more than five years experience with the technology. Conversely, only three of the officers interviewed had any polygraph experience.

Agencies that had discontinued use of the polygraph had done so, according to survey results, an average of ten years earlier and only 15 percent of the agencies surveyed still used polygraph but had no preference for either technology.

Twenty percent of the agencies had discontinued the use of polygraph in favor of CVSA®, because they believed the technology was more reliable; 35 percent said polygraph was too expensive to own and operate; 50 percent said polygraph operators were hard to schedule; and 50 percent said they dropped polygraph in order to gravitate to newer technology.

The primary uses for polygraph and CVSA® were for criminal investigations and background checks, survey respondents reported. Far less often, they were used for covert investigations and other purposes.

Because the average perceived reliability of CVSA® among survey respondents ranged from 80 to 100 percent (average = 91.38 percent), it likely came as no surprise to those reviewing the survey results that general comments about CVSA® were positive (i.e., "Benefit to their organization," "Helped GREATLY to SOLVE CRIMES," and "CRITICAL TOOL").

The survey's "Conclusions" section included more pro-CVSA® statements -- including "Can save valuable time in tactical situations," "Can save lives" and "No threat to polygraph" -- and SOCOM leaders told NITV officials they were 100 percent committed to the project.

* * *

With survey results in hand, SOCOM officials faced only one more hurdle in the form of Carol A. Haave, a Deputy Under Secretary of Defense (DUSD) under Cambone who oversaw CIFA, the agency in charge of DoD polygraph programs, and the Defense Security Service (DSS), responsible for granting top-secret security clearances.

Not surprisingly, a number of government watchdogs, journalists, and others before me have scrutinized Haave's work. Among them, officials at The Center for Public Integrity published some interesting findings about her in an article[28] October 30, 2003.

For starters, they reported Haave was a principal at a defense contractor, Sullivan Haave Associates (SHA), along with her husband, Terry Sullivan; SHA won DoD contracts worth $78,000 in 1999, for providing "basic services' to the Defense Advanced Research Projects Agency (DARPA), and $100,000 in 2001, for providing "technical services" to the Army.

In addition, they reported Sullivan insisted he and his wife kept her work at the Pentagon separate from his work at SHA.

Toward the end of the article, they cited a "biography posted on the Web site of a Pentagon advisory group she met with in July" which reportedly described Sullivan Haave Associates "as having been a 'woman-owned company that operated solely on behalf of the Department of Defense to facilitate the transition of advanced technologies into military operations.'"

Reminds one of the saying, "having your cake, and eating it, too."

In his book[29], *Feasting on the Spoils: The Life and Times of Randy "Duke" Cunningham, History's Most Corrupt Congressman*, author Seth Hettena devoted significant time and attention to Haave's association with Mitchell Wade, the defense contractor at the center of the bribery scandal that saw the book's title character receive an eight-year prison sentence.

NITV's Humble expressed concerns about Haave, too.

Before a notary March 2, 2005, Humble signed an affidavit in which he affirmed several things to be true.

In the document, Humble recalled speaking with Andy Poole, one of the SOCOM officials with whom he was working on the FIST project, February 28, 2005, about a discussion Poole had had with Haave about the possible use of the CVSA® by SOCOM.

Poole, according to Humble's affidavit, told the NITV executive his discussion with Haave included talk about a CVSA®-focused study Cambone had commissioned at the University of Florida (UF). Likewise, Poole told Humble that, during the discussion, Haave stated, "I already know how that is going to come out."

That statement, according to the affidavit, implies Haave "has knowledge as to what the results will be before that study is conducted."

If true, Haave's statement becomes problematic when one considers the fact that the UF study's results were still more than a year from publication at the time Humble signed his affidavit.

\* \* \*

Several high-level conversations, including several that took the form of email exchanges, followed.

On April 29, 2005, Lindsey Neas forwarded an email message to Humble. It included the language his boss, Senator Jim Talent of Missouri, requested be placed into the language of an SASC bill:

The committee is aware that there are competing interrogative technologies being used in both the military intelligence and law enforcement communities with varying degrees of efficacy. The committee believe that the demands placed on both communities, particularly by the ongoing Global War on Terrorism, necessitate the adoption of a policy by the Secretary of Defense that would allow personnel across the Department of Defense to use and adopt those interrogative tools they have found to be most effective. While the polygraph has for years served as the benchmark used by military and law enforcement personnel, the committee is increasingly aware of newer technologies, including voice stress analysis, which are yielding promising results. Field reports over the past two years demonstrate a significant ability to distinguish between a suspect's truthful and false statements and the ability to identify false positive statements. Similar positive reports have been received from various metropolitan police departments around the country. The committee is encouraged by these findings and, thereby, directs the Secretary of Defense to promulgate a policy across the Department, effective upon the date of enactment, permitting personnel to employ the interrogative technologies, including both the polygraph and voice stress analysis, which they believe to be most effective.

Three days later, Humble shared a message about the same subject with more than two-dozen high-level Senate staffers, most of whom were military liaisons.

"I met with quite a few senators at the Senatorial Trust meeting in Washington Thursday and Friday and we discussed the language that Senator Talent has introduced into the Senate Armed Services Committee," Humble's message began.

"As you are aware, the polygraphers from the Department of Defense Polygraph Institute (DoDPI), working through CIFA, have been using every tool at their disposal, including distortions of the truth as well as outright lies, to stop DoD agencies *[sic]* from acquiring the Computer Voice Stress Analyzer (CVSA). However, because of the dramatic success of the CVSA both in the U.S. law enforcement community as well as in Iraq and GTMO (we now have a full-time staff member assigned there as a Subject Matter Expert on a two-year *[sic]* contract), it is becoming increasingly difficult for them (DoDPI & CIFA) to justify their position. However, DoDPI is still strongly resisting the technology as it eliminates the need for the old polygraph and, their positions. However, we are all aware that it is imperative that we supply our troops in the field with the very best in field-proven technology, regardless of whose 'rice bowl' is broken. To this end, Senator Talent has introduced the attached wording which simply gives DoD entities the choice of which investigative/interrogation tool to utilize and when to utilize it. The wording does not require anyone to acquire the system nor does it require the expenditure of monies.

"Since time is of the essence, it is important that each senator's military liaison contact Deputy Staff Director Bill Greenwalt and express their senator's support for the language. If possible, Lindsey (Senator Talent's Military Liaison) has asked that each senator's ML make the call no later than Wednesday.

"Although I will miss communicating with you on a regular basis, should this wording pass, it will end the years of hard work that many of us put into this battle, especially Senators Inhofe and Allen, to name a few."

Nine days later, Greenwalt received a message from James Pitchford. Not only did it contain news that Pitchford's boss, Senator Christopher "Kit" Bond of Missouri, was backing the bill, but it contained a statement about how the longtime senator, a member of the Senate Intelligence Committee, felt about the folks at Polygraph Headquarters.

"Like Senator Talent," Pitchford wrote, "Senator Bond cannot understand how DoDPI & CIFA can continue to justify their position opposing the use of this technology."

Within 48 hours, according to a message one SOCOM official sent to two colleagues May 13, 2005, a large number of SASC senators joined Senators Talent and Bond in supporting the language.

"The below emails show SASC support for CVSA and the Field Interrogation Support Tool (FIST). Senators [sic] Bond and Talent along with twenty other Senator's (highlighted in red below) will endorse language to be included in this year's [sic] defense bill supporting both the polygraph and voice stress analysis. This language (last email/key points highlighted in blue), to be effective upon the date of enactment, would direct SECDEF to promulgate a policy across the Department permitting personnel to employ the interrogative technologies which they believe to be most effective.

"As you know, todays video conference [sic] with Ms. Haave was cancelled for the second time and rescheduled for May 25th. This approach (multiple folks involved) may be too hard to accomplish. Would it be possible for you to call Ms.

94

Haave and gain her support for SOCOM to move forward with the FIST Defense Acquisition Challenge Program?"

Not surprisingly, the already-twice-cancelled video conference was cancelled again -- permanently -- and Cambone proved SOCOM leaders' fears accurate. In mid-June 2005, he ordered SOCOM leaders to cancel the FIST project just as it was set to launch.

Three months later, Humble sent an email message to a number of congressional staffers. In addition to showing Humble was concerned about Haave's involvement with SHA, the text of his message, dated September 15, 2005, contained an interesting question.

"Why would a Deputy Under Secretary of Defense, after she received a read-ahead packet regarding an independent survey commissioned by SOCOM (Dr. Gallagher's survey) that established the perceived accuracy of the CVSA in the law enforcement community and from military CVSA examiners at 91%, refuse three briefings on the SOCOM survey?" Humble wrote. "And, why would she then order the $690,000.00 in R&D monies that had already been approved and sent to SOCOM to enhance the CVSA returned to her office? And finally, why did her office direct that everyone at SOCOM not to have any further contact with your company?

"We are concerned that Sullivan Haave Associates may be involved with a competing technology," Humble continued. "If Carol Haave allowed the SOCOM project involving the CVSA to move forward, which very nearly happened, Sullivan Haave may have lost future business in its stated area of expertise 'advanced technologies.' Is there any other explanation as to why already approved R&D monies to enhance a technology that is currently used by more than 1,400 law enforcement agencies and the US military (before Carol Haave's intervention) was ordered returned by Carol Haave without explanation?

"We have also learned that Sullivan Haave has been investigated previously by the DoD Inspector General (Contract Number DASW01-03-F-0516)," Humble continued. "Also, as I recently advised you, the $690,000 that was earmarked for our project mysteriously disappeared and is now at the center of a bribery/kick-back scandal involving SOCOM. There are too many unanswered questions involving the actions of Carol Haave, Sullivan Haave Associates, and the SOCOM scandal to be left unaddressed."

Though it's unclear as to exactly what conversations took place, it quickly became apparent to NITV officials that Cambone and Haave succeeded in convincing General Bryan D. "Doug" Brown, SOCOM commander, to shut down the FIST project.

NITV officials knew they had lost the FIST fight (no pun intended), but they did not stop fighting the turf war.

# CHAPTER TEN:
# Polygraph Fails in Iraq

While CVSA® was experiencing setbacks at home, the polygraph experienced something of a setback overseas. Incredibly, a survey of U.S. Air Force polygraph examiners who were involved in conducting those tests yielded results showing polygraph no more effective than flipping a coin.

From August 1, 2004, to October 15, 2006, the USAF Polygraph Program conducted Relevant/Irrelevant Screening Tests (R/IST) on detainees in the Iraqi theater of operations, according to the document, "TALKING PAPER ON SCREENING TEST FOR DETAINEE OPERATIONS,"[30] which contained the survey results.

Appearing atop 50 talking-paper pages, the front page of the redacted document contained bullet points highlighting the results of surveys.

Notable among those results found after conducting polygraph tests on 768 detainees was the finding that "detainee personnel are just as likely to have committed the suspected act as not." That finding stemmed from the fact that 47 percent of the tests yielded "No Deception Indicated" results while 46 percent yielded "Deception Indicated" and seven percent "No Opinion."

Though the overwhelming majority of polygraph examinations were requested to determine a detainee's involvement in multiple acts of anti-coalition force activity (i.e., weapons smuggling, IED making, armed attack against coalition forces, membership/association with insurgent groups, etc.), survey results showed that only ten percent of the requests for polygraph support contained sufficiently-detailed information for the conduct of specific-issue exams currently utilized by the USAF Polygraph Program.

Additionally, survey results showed that 90 percent of the tests were, by definition, "screening examinations wherein the examiner is called to resolve numerous and divergent issues based on extremely generic, anonymous, and perishable reporting."

Those exams were conducted, according to the talking paper, despite the fact that Air Force Office of Special Investigations (AFOSI) Instruction 71-103, Vol. 7, 29 Aug 2000, does not authorize the use of a polygraph technique suitable for the screening of detainee personnel who are potentially involved in multiple unrelated, unsubstantiated, and wide-ranging acts against coalition forces.

A quarter of the polygraph examiners surveyed pointed out problems posed by language barriers.

"The Arabic language itself presents an obstacle due to the different translations and dialect and at times the wrong translation of the question was noted by other interpreters," one examiner said.

"Many interpreters were not fluent in the written Arabic language, precluding them being used by polygraph," another reported. "They could not translate questions from English to Arabic and back again."

"I was fortunate to have had motivated interpreters," a third responded. "Without them we can't do the job (without language/culture knowledge)."

A fourth examiner reported, "there was definitely a difference in the level of interpreter experience. Some knew the language and some had a hard time."

Remember, as reported earlier in this book, CVSA® was used at GITMO more than 90 times and achieved a success rate -- defined as developing new, previously-unknown intelligence which was independently confirmed or confirmed existing information that otherwise could not be verified -- of 92 percent despite the fact most exams were conducted using interpreters.

# CHAPTER ELEVEN:
## 'Hey Guy...'

Though it remains unclear as to exactly how and when the initial connection was made, it became apparent during my investigation that DoD polygraph officials had reached out to their counterparts at the National Institute of Justice (NIJ) for help during the early months of 2005 -- at about the same time SOCOM survey results were being firmed up.

Why did DoD polygraph officials reach out to NIJ, the Department of Justice's (DoJ) research, development, and evaluation arm? Perhaps, because they believed attacking CVSA® on multiple fronts would yield the best results.

After DoD officials reached out to them, NIJ officials reached out to University of Oklahoma Professor Kelly R. Damphousse (pronounced "dam-foos") March 29, 2005.

With two tiny words in a mid-afternoon email message, the ball started rolling on the NIJ-funded research project that would result, two years later, in publication of a 127-page research report, "Assessing the Validity of Voice Stress Analysis Tools in a Jail Setting (a.k.a., 'The Oklahoma Study')."[31]

Using FOIA and the Oklahoma Open Records Act, I was able to read those two words as well as thousands of others contained in hundreds of messages and correspondence exchanged about The Oklahoma Study.

"Hey guy," wrote Christine Crossland, an NIJ senior social science analyst. "I left you a voice message on your direct line for the Dean's office. Where are you? Are we working banker hours these days."

Writing from her office in the 800 block of Seventh Street, NW, in the nation's capitol, Crossland went on to ask Professor Damphousse -- then a middle-aged assistant professor of sociology and rising star among faculty members in the university's College of Arts and Sciences -- if he would have time the following day to "talk shop."

"I would really like to work with you and crew using an ADAM[32] model of data collection (using arrestees) to test/validate an Office of Science and Technology (OS&T) toy--the Voice Stress Analyzer (VSA)," she wrote.

"I'm looking at collecting 300 workable samples," Crossland continued. "I had originally thought of using two sites but looking at the 2003 and 2004 ADAM data, OKC and Tulsa could serve as the two sites. We'd pay for you, the site coordinators, and me to be trained by the vendor on the VSA equipment. NOTE: Training location to be determined but OS&T folks are talking about the mountains of Oregon some time in Aug/Sept."

Crossland went on to outline what she envisioned as a project timeline, noting a July-August window for completion of the project's final report, before closing with a cordial message, "Look forward to working with you fellow. Take care."

Following that initial message, I was able to uncover much of what transpired during the two years and two days that followed.

The first noteworthy message was sent, no foolin', April 1, 2005, at 3:10 p.m. It took the form of a cautiously-optimistic e-mail message from Professor Damphousse to his wife, Beth, and two other women -- Laura J. Pointon and Deidra Upchurch -- who had worked with him on the aforementioned ADAM projects.

"We might be back in business (at least for a bit)," he wrote. "Let me know if you are interested. Please treat this as confidential information for now. Kelly."

A short time passed and, after apparently failing to connect with her by phone, Professor Damphousse replied to Crossland via email.

"Just FYI, I am interested (sorry we are failing to hook up)," he wrote before asking her to call him.

During the next couple of months, more electronic messages were exchanged between Professor Damphousse and Crossland, and both attended a hastily-arranged "vendors meeting" in Washington, D.C., in early May 2005. Also in attendance were representatives of V-Worldwide and NITV, the two companies whose equipment would be the focus of the professor and his team of researchers -- that is, once they received funding to conduct The Oklahoma Study.

A few days after the meeting ended and approximately seven weeks after her first mention of The Oklahoma Study to Professor Damphousse, Crossland began sharing more details about the proposed project.

"Hey guy," she wrote in an early-morning message May 18, 2005. "I just wanted to say thank you, thank you, thank you. I really appreciate you coming to town on late notice and participating at the vendor's meetings. It sounds like an interesting and exciting project where we can expand our domain, so to speak, into the realm of science and technology-- or, as I like to call it, the boys with toys division (har, har)."

In the next paragraph, she asked Professor Damphousse if he could start working on and thinking about the budget for his end of the work. In addition, she let him know that lab costs for the project would fall under his purview as well.

The professor responded by asking Crossland how long the written proposal should be and if there was a cost limit.

"Whatever it takes to cover everything so external peer reviewers can review it," Crossland replied. "I'll have two researchers and one practitioner review it--between 12-15 pages or more, if necessary. Remember that these reviewers don't know ADAM methodology so it may take more space to explain the population, conditions, and so forth. The budget is up to you. It's the same for the grant, include travel, training, consultants, if necessary, the lab fees (!), data collection, and so on. I've got 300K but I need at least 50K for other project related costs. I'd recommend no more than 150-175 unless you really need more. Try not to exceed 200K."

Whatever it takes? Professor Damphousse came up with a draft grant proposal with a total dollar amount, $177,921.

In an early-morning message June 15, 2005, he forwarded his draft grant proposal to Rebecca K. "Becki" Moore, a grant writer and statistician employed by the Oklahoma Department of Mental Health and Substance Abuse Services (ODMHSAS) in Oklahoma City. Interestingly, Moore -- instead of Professor Damphousse -- would end up being listed on the project's Budget Detail Worksheet as "lead investigator."

Contained in his message to Moore, Professor Damphousse's description of events related to the draft proposal brings to mind the image of a college student cramming for a final exam rather than a professor seeking a grant worth close to $200,000.

"Yes, it really is 5:33 and I did stay up all night," he wrote. "This is probably a mush heap but I didn't get to start it until 3 or so. If you can't make heads or tails of it, PLEASE call me.

"You will likely need to re-work the letter," his message continued. "It's just a draft. I'm not good at writing those things but it is the least I can do. If you want a greater hand in this project, please know that you are welcome. I just don't want to push something on you. Thanks Becki. Kel."

Remarkably, the proposal letter -- which, by Professor Damphousse's own admission, took him less than three hours to prepare -- was edited by Moore, printed on ODMHSAS letterhead, signed by Stephen Davis, Ph.D. -- then director of the agency's Decision Support Services section and the professor's primary point of contact at the state agency -- and forwarded to Crossland at her Washington, D.C., office the same day.

Also remarkable, but in a different way, were four words, Investigator Initiated Research Proposal, that appeared atop the title page of the proposal packet accompanying the letter.

In order to believe the proposal was initiated by anyone other than NIJ's Crossland, one would have to ignore the email messages two months earlier that showed Crossland -- not Dr. Davis, Professor Damphousse, or anyone in Oklahoma -- was behind the project's launch.

Moving on.

Outlined in the proposal was $157,452 in estimated direct costs that included items such as salaries and wages, fringe benefits, travel, and subcontract(s). Also included were estimated indirect costs, a standard 13 percent rate charged by the state agency, totaling $20,469.

Combined, the total estimated cost of the proposal -- again, $177,921 -- was projected to cover all costs during the proposed research period, September 1, 2005, to July 31, 2006.

The majority of costs listed in the proposal fell under the "Consultant/Contracts" section where I learned ODMHSAS would contract with KayTen Research and Development LLC ("KayTen"), a limited-liability company based in Norman, Oklahoma.

KayTen, in turn, would "provide assistance to this project by (1) serving as a liaison with VSA vendors, (2) obtaining training for data collectors in VSA procedures, (3) collecting data for the project, (4) ensuring that urine samples are sent to analysis company in a timely manner, (5) conducting data analysis procedures, (6) writing technical reports, and (7) presenting findings at national research conferences." The total cost for the subcontract was listed as $150,544.

Notable among items listed under the estimate of direct costs was an entry explaining that Dr. Davis would not be seeking funding for his salary via the proposal and, instead, would provide his effort "in kind."

In the final paragraph of the proposal's cover letter, addressed to Crossland and dated June 15, 2005, was another interesting collection of words.

"This proposal is not a response to a specific RFP from NIJ, but the Department hopes you will consider this a study worthy of funding."

Again, while Dr. Davis was truthful in describing the proposal as not being a response to a specific Request for Proposal from NIJ, acceptance of that statement at face value requires one to forget the content of the messages dating back to March 29, 2005, when Crossland opened her message to Professor Damphousse with the salutation, "Hey guy."

Once in the hands of NIJ officials, the proposal was reviewed by one internal and two external practitioners. In turn, Professor Damphousse was given a chance to counter any criticism. Only after that step could it be approved for funding.

While the internal reviewer threw mostly "softball" concerns at the professor, the external practitioners raised several worthwhile issues.

"If there is a positive outcome to the validity of the VSA for detecting deception," wrote external practitioner #1, "this non-invasive tool can be applied to all aspects of the justice system, from arrest to treatment to the courtroom (i.e. drug courts)," he wrote. "It can be used within treatment programs in jails and prisons such as sex offender and drug/alcohol programs. Eventually it could take the place of urine analysis if tested and proven as a standard for judges. Polygraphs are not admissible as evidence in courts to date -- is this a breakthrough technology?"

Professor Damphousse countered those remarks and others that accompanied them in a message to Crossland sent July 13, 2005, at 12:32 a.m.

"THE technology is new but still in its infancy," he wrote. "Polygraph has been around for over 100 years and is not admissible *[sic]*. I don't seen VSA as gaining acceptance soon. On the other hand, law enforcement still uses it as an investigative tool. The point is, does it work? Should we be spending millions on it?"

Apparently, the professor did not know voice stress technology was not "new." The precursor to it had, after all, been developed almost four decades earlier by Colonel Bell and his colleagues, and it had taken a giant leap forward in the form of CVSA®.

Among the observations shared by external practitioner #2 was a concern about urinalysis testing.

"The final decision as to whether deception or truthfulness is verified will be based on urinalysis testing ("ground testing"), in itself less than fool proof, and problematic," he wrote.

"I don't follow this," Professor Damphousse answered. "If I had more time, I was going to add some analyses that I once did about lying using OKC ADAM data. I would have been clear about the problems of using drug testing as proof of recent drug use (e.g., THC and meth have different metabolism rates). I think that drug testing provides pretty good grounding."

Regarding the potential impact of the proposed project, external reviewer #2 offered comments that were probably not warmly received by his part-time paymaster, NIJ.

"The proposal does not provide any avenues of advancement in the scientific or technical processes that utilize technology to detect deception or truthfulness," he wrote, "nor does it lead criminal justice or substance abuse services in any direction that would enhance their existing techniques."

"I don't agree," the professor replied. "Law enforcement is starting to invest heavily into VSA and we don't have any idea if it works. Indeed, all the evidence that we have actually shows that it does not work."

Adding to his criticism, external practitioner #2 wrote that the proposal "does not indicate any cost savings would occur, but actually be in addition to existing programs unless proof in the validity of one or both of the VSA software program test results are established."

In response, Professor Damphousse seemed to focus only on the likelihood CVSA® would be proven a failure.

"Again, the cost savings would be if we show that VSA does NOT work," the professor wrote, "then law enforcement can stop spending money on the products."

"In conclusion," external practitioner #2 noted, "the applicant has identified several areas of concern why a great deal of work needs to be done to validate VSA testing technology. As this project is written, it would verify the mentioned areas of concern but did not offer any potential solutions."

That note prompted a one-line response from Professor Damphousse.

"Just knowing if VSA works or not will be a major advance," he wrote.

If the reviewers had seen the content of an email message Professor Damphousse had sent to Crossland eight days earlier, they might have gained more insight into the professor's thinking as he prepared to conduct the study.

"Actually this is all part of the national drama between Polygraph and the VSA folks," wrote Professor Damphousse as part of an electronic conversation with Crossland about the seemingly-difficult process of obtaining approval from the Oklahoma Board of Polygraph Examiners for the data-collection portion of the study to be conducted in Oklahoma City. "The polygraph people are fearful that VSA will put them out of business...."

I repeat: Professor Damphousse wrote, "The polygraph people are fearful that VSA will put them out of business...."

Little did the professor realize, his words stood as confirmation of what Colonel Bell had written a quarter-century earlier about three options -- in particular, the third option (i.e., "...they could attempt to ensure the survival of the polygraph by eliminating the challenger") -- available to polygraph loyalists as CVSA® technology gained more and more acceptance.

Professor Damphousse went on to characterize the ongoing debate between polygraph loyalists and CVSA® advocates as "one pseudo science freaked out by another pseudo science" before sharing some interesting commentary about polygraph officials in Oklahoma.

"They are happy to see research that shows VSA doesn't work - they just don't want research that shows that VSA DOES work," the professor wrote."

Barely 14 hours after receiving Professor Damphousse's responses to the reviewers' comments, Crossland replied with a message, the subject line of which told him all he needed to know: "GMS App Approval has been completed!" The quick turnaround revealed NIJ's review-and-rebuttal process was little more than an exercise in paperwork.

The proposal had been approved via NIJ's Grant Management System (GMS), and the professor could "start uploading documents for App#2005-93554-OK-IJ."

Professor Damphousse replied to Crossland's e-mail just after 10 o'clock that evening, informing her that the task of submitting documents via GMS had been completed by Moore, ending with, "I hope, I hope, I hope..."

Crossland sent another message to the professor and Moore early the next morning. In it, she confirmed she had "checked it out and it all looks good" -- and that wasn't all!

Under the words, "Next steps," she offered a strong hint that more money had become available for the project.

"Can you and Becky start working on a revised budget?" Crossland wrote. "I'm still confirming with my partners in OS&T about funds but I think you have $232,200 to work with."

The NIJ official went on to explain that the increased costs (i.e., $54,279) "should cover (1) female data collection; (2) the two vendors or law enforcement agents hired and already trained on the VSA to conduct analyses; (3) reports, and (4) increased staff time to cover analyses, data collection, etc. If you feel it necessary, you can add consultant time (VSA expertise) but that's up to you."

Only five days later, a revised proposal -- five pages (including cover) -- was faxed from Dr. Davis' office at ODMHSAS to Crossland's office at NIJ.

The revised proposal's breakout of costs included few changes in most areas, but increases totaling $47,985 in the "Consultants/Contracts" category.

Notable among those increases were: $14,800 added to the cost of KayTen's services; $20,000 added to cover costs to hire two experts (to be recommended by each of the vendors) to perform voice stress analyses (200 exams at $50 each) on the data once it was collected; and $13,185 added to cover costs related to ODMHSAS subcontracting with "an expert in performing psychometric data analyses" who would "have experience in performing analyses related to testing for deception."

Combined with $6,244 in indirect costs, the changes increased the proposal's dollar amount by $54,279 and brought the bottom-line to $232,200, aligning perfectly with the amount

Crossland had told Professor Damphousse was available days earlier.

The revised proposal's Budget Detail Worksheet, that would cover the period September 1, 2005, to July 31, 2006, provided a look at how KayTen planned to spend the $165,344 it would be allotted via the grant.

Notable among proposed costs were: $49,000 for Professor Damphousse's salary and wages; $56,203 for laptops, software and training from the vendors (V-Worldwide = $39,000 and NITV = $17,203); and $15,000 ($20 per hour x 750 hours of work) for interviewers' salaries and wages.

In addition, the revised proposal included: $11,711 in "fringe benefits" for study personnel; $10,260 ($19 per hour x 540 hours) for jail security officers; $6,180 for estimated travel costs; $5,000 for lab tests ($5,000); and $5,000 for an office manager.

Seventy days after the initial proposal was approved and 64 days after the revised proposal was submitted, DOJ's Office of Justice Programs sent a fax to then-U.S. Rep. Ernest Istook (R-Okla.). Dated September 21, 2005, it contained the less-than-surprising news that NIJ had awarded $232,200 to ODMHSAS for The Oklahoma Study.

* * *

Before data collection for the study could begin, Professor Damphousse had to hire staff to be trained to conduct examinations with both types of voice stress devices. Not surprisingly, he hired Pointon and Upchurch. In addition, he added his wife Beth to the payroll.

After working out logistical concerns, Pointon and Upchurch would travel together to NITV headquarters in

Florida and to a V-Worldwide facility in Waupun, Wisconsin, for hands-on training with each company's technology.

Training took place in Florida the week of November 14, 2005, and then Pointon and Upchurch returned to Oklahoma to work with Moore on two important tasks -- lining up a lab to test urine samples collected from jail inmates and scheduling testing dates at the Oklahoma County Jail in Oklahoma City. Before making much progress, however, the trio experienced professional and personal difficulties.

On December 2, 2005, Moore sent an acronym-filled email message to Crossland and copied Professor Damphousse.

"We are not having the best of luck with labs," Moore wrote. "STL no longer does NIDA-5 testing; Quest Diagnostics wants $67.40 per sample; Abbott labs doesn't do testing, they only provide kits; and PharmChem has a letter to their creditors on the website discussing their liquidation. Do you have any other suggestions?"

This stood as the first indication costs might trump accuracy in the process researchers used to select a method for testing urine for the presence of drugs.

On December 12, 2005, at 7:07 a.m., Crossland sent an email to both Professor Damphousse and Moore.

"Someone recommended to me that due to the prohibitive costs of doing off-site drug testing," Crossland wrote, "that you all might want to consider onsite drug testing instead. Initially, I was concerned about the confirmation of methamphetamine but I was told tests now exist that can test for the drug. I have found a company that claims to be able to test for it in their kit.

"If you chose to go this route," she continued, "you could (1) test all samples on site or (2) test all samples on site and only send the amphetamine/meth positives to be tested. The former would be less costly. Given that these results are being used for a research purposes only, it might be more prudent to go this route."

Crossland cited "the small sample numbers used" as the main reason why companies were charging so much to conduct the urine tests. Before closing her message, she promised to send information about one company's kits for review and consideration via FedEx®.

Eight hours later, Professor Damphousse sent an email to Pointon regarding training and data collection.

"Tentatively," he wrote, "we are going to pilot the project on Feb 5&6 (Sunday and Monday). Then, we will collect data for 14 days following that. We will probably not be mailing pee. We will likely do the test on-site (long story having mostly to do with cost). I don't think that it will be too much of a hassle (I hope)."

Via that message, the professor appeared to confirm that his choice of a urinalysis-testing tool -- the one he previously said, "provides pretty good grounding" -- was based largely on costs rather than accuracy.

In a message to Pointon seven minutes later, Professor Damphousse gave the researcher an assignment.

"Will you start doing that thing you do so well (call your jail buddies to see if we can come play)?" he asked.

Pointon replied at 3:12 p.m., writing, "I'll *[sic]* talk to Deidra about the times and we will let you know but I assume that will be fine. I'll start calling ASAP and talking to my peeps!!"

Unfortunately for the research team, more roadblocks surfaced as Christmas 2005 approached.

First, emails were exchanged between Crossland and the researchers, and a decision was made December 22, 2005, to push back the training at V-Worldwide by one day. Why? Because the Super Bowl was set to take place February 5, 2006. The schedule change would result in the first date for data collection being pushed back 20 days as well.

Next, Crossland sent a curious and brief message to Professor Damphousse December 29, 2005. In it, she let him know she had received an offer of assistance from a small group of individuals at the Northeast Law Enforcement Analysis Facility (LEAF) in Rome, New York -- people who had produced an NIJ-funded study, "Investigation and Evaluation of Voice Stress Analysis Technology,"[33] on voice stress four years earlier.

"The gentlemen below have been trying to 'get involved' in the VSA project," Crossland wrote. "For reasons I cannot explain now, it is important that they do not get involved. If they should get a hold of you, you can reiterate my comments below -- in other words, thanks, but no thanks."

\* \* \*

Why did Crossland *not* want LEAF researchers involved? Though she refused to respond to repeated inquiries on that subject, I suspect it had something to do with the fact that some of the people at LEAF had been involved in the aforementioned study in which CVSA® was not involved.

Published March 20, 2002, that study's "CONCLUSIONS" section contained the statement, "After reviewing the three technical tests performed, it could be stated that VSA units do recognize stress."

Furthermore, the authors indicated in the "SUGGESTED FOLLOW ON" section of the study that LEAF folks should be involved in future research "because of their extensive VSA background."

Rather than involve people with "extensive VSA background" who seemed interested in looking at CVSA®, Crossland appears to have wanted to ensure The Oklahoma Study was conducted only by people who, for the most part, were unfamiliar with voice stress technology *and* had proven themselves reliable in previous NIJ-funded research efforts. People like Professor Damphousse and his team of researchers, perhaps?

* * *

On the third day of 2006, yet another difficulty surfaced in the form of an email message from Pointon to the professor. In it, the sender explained, "a few unfortunate developments over the Christmas break that may impact the beginning of the project" and prevent her from traveling to Wisconsin for training. Those developments involved illnesses of elderly members in both Pointon's and Upchurch's families.

While both situations were unfortunate, it was Pointon's that pushed her to display what could be interpreted either as a sign of naiveté or simply as sheer ignorance about the task at hand.

After offering more details about her situation, Pointon wrote, "I know if Deidra were to go that she could train me adequately when she returns but I'm not sure if this will be okay with all others involved."

Apparently, Pointon believed Upchurch could, upon receiving training on the non-polygraph equipment, train her to operate and understand that equipment in a manner equal to the training offered by vendor representatives with years of experience.

Despite all of the difficulties and dire circumstances, both Pointon and Upchurch somehow managed to complete their training so that, months later, the project could move into the data-collection phase.

Only days before that phase began, email records show NIJ officials received an inquiry from producers of the ABC News program, *Primetime*, who were interested in NIJ-funded voice stress research. Perhaps that was the DoD-NIJ connection?

On February 23, 2006, John Morgan, NIJ's OS&T director, sent a message to Michael O'Shea, program manager for the agency's Operational Technologies Division, and Crossland. He asked them to help the folks in NIJ's Office of Communications (OCOM).

"We have an inquiry from ABC News concerning our voice stress research," Morgan wrote. "Can you all put together a paragraph or two to update the Oklahoma study for Catherine Saunders down in OCOM? Thanks."

In a response to Morgan, O'Shea and others, Crossland seemed less than eager to provide details.

"I'm not exactly clear what ABC wants or already knows about this project," she wrote. "I'm also uneasy about releasing this information for national release while we are in the midst of data collection. After all, arrestees do watch TV, especially while they are in jail. That said, this news article could adversely affect response rates."

After noting she had included a project description and background with her message, Crossland went on to explain that the project was "currently in the data collection phase" and that a draft report was not expected until late summer 2006 with public dissemination scheduled for sometime in the fall 2006.

The next day, NIJ Spokesperson Catherine Sanders responded to Crossland's message with an update for all addressees.

"Just heard back from ABC," Sanders wrote. "Primetime is doing a story on CVSA and wants to make sure they are aware of all research that has been done on it. She mentioned a 2000 report.

"Christine -- we would not release any unfinished report before data is collected," she continued, "so we won't mention the report you reference below. But is there anything else that ABC should be aware of?"

Though I could not determine whether or not Crossland had responded to that question from Sanders, I did see she sent Professor Damphousse a message early the next morning.

"Heads up...we'll discuss when I get there," Crossland wrote just before 7 a.m. February 25, 2006. "I'm heading to the airport in about an hour."

It's impossible to know exactly what Crossland and Damphousse discussed during their in-person meeting; regardless, data collection began the following day.

* * *

"On February 26, 2006," according to the narrative on page 29 of The Oklahoma Study, "the research team entered the jail for the first time to practice using the equipment in the jail facility. Our original plan was to collect data using both LVA[34] and CVSA at the same time but we discovered that our

118

data collection room (a small office just outside of booking) was too small to allow for two interviews to be conducted at the same time. As a result, we collected data using the CVSA program for the first 12 days and then using the LVA program for the second 12 days...."

"We successfully tested our protocol again on February 27 and then began data collection in earnest on February 28 and concluded March 24, 2006. We only include data collected from February 28 through March 24 in our analyses. We took one day off between the CVSA data collection (February 28-March 13, 2006) and the LVA data collection (March 15-March 24, 2006). Only two surveys were collected on March 20 because one of the interviewers became ill."

After outlining how data collection took place, the researchers described in more detail how they had told each inmate prior to his exam that: (1) the interview could not be used to harm him in any way during his stay in the facility or at a later date; (2) participation was voluntary; and (3) responses would be recorded to test how well the technologies determined stress.

In short, they explained to each inmate that his participation in the research project would involve no real-life jeopardy.

Interviews were conducted with each taking 15 to 30 minutes to complete, according to the report. Afterward, each subject was asked to complete the data-collection process by supplying a urine specimen.

"If the subject agreed," the report continued, "he was escorted to a private restroom where he was asked to fill a specimen bottle with his urine. The interviewers were trained to recognize and respond to respondents who returned specimen bottles returned with water or diluted urine. All urine samples contained sufficient urine to be able to perform a drug test. Those arrestees who completed the interview and provided a urine sample were given a candy bar as an incentive."

"After the first few days of data collection with CVSA," the report noted, "the research team sent copies of the output files to the CVSA expert to make certain that the data was being collected correctly. Other than some problems with over-modulation, we were assured that all was well and we proceeded to collect the data."

Later in the report, the researchers used a variant of "successful" to describe their data collection efforts, but not the performance of the non-polygraph technologies involved in the study.

"The results are not promising," the researchers reported, later adding, "both programs failed consistently to correctly identify respondents who were being deceptive."

Four months after completing their CVSA® training in Florida, the researchers wrapped up two weeks of data collection in Oklahoma City. After that, another four more months passed before any new or noteworthy communications were exchanged between the Oklahoma researchers and Crossland.

# CHAPTER TWELVE:
# 'Dear Senator Santorum...'

In addition to issuing his memo and clamping down on SOCOM, Cambone issued a call for a "DoD sponsored independent study" to "assess the reliability of VSA." Before the study took place, however, he sent a letter to U.S. Senator Rick Santorum. It was in the body of that letter that I became aware of the existence of The Cambone Memo.

While Cambone's letter to the Pennsylvania Republican bore an ink-stamp date of August 26 in its upper-right corner, the four digits representing the year of its origin were smeared beyond recognition in the copy of the letter I obtained. Based upon other information and documents available to me, however, I concluded the letter had been written in 2004.

Obtained from a confidential source, the content of the letter suggests Cambone wrote it as a reply to an inquiry Senator Santorum had made about voice stress technology sometime earlier.

While it remains unclear exactly what prompted the senator to request information from Cambone, it takes a reader very little time to understand the objective of Cambone's reply to Senator Santorum.

In short, it appears Cambone wanted to bring an end to the wave of positive publicity CVSA® had been receiving as a result of its successes at GITMO, in Iraq and elsewhere.

After telling the senator he appreciated the opportunity to respond to his request for information about the use of voice stress systems for military purposes, Cambone launched into a polite effort via which he appeared to want to convince the senator that things were under control and he should buzz off.

"The DoD must establish effective procedures and standards for verifying sources and validating intelligence information," Cambone began. "In doing so, we look to leverage only technologies with a firm scientific foundation. In a memorandum dated June 8, 2004, I provided interim policy that until the accuracy of other technologies could be supported by independent scientific research, the polygraph is the only instrument approved in the DoD for use as a credibility assessment tool. That guidance was based on analysis such as that by the National Research Council (NRC), which operates under a charter granted by Congress.

"After reviewing thirty years of evaluations on VSA," he continued, "the NRC issued a report in 2002 concluding that the research offered 'little or no scientific basis for the use of the computer voice stress analyzer or similar voice measurement instruments.' The NRC report observed that, 'Although proponents of voice stress analysis claim high levels of accuracy, empirical research on the validity of the technique has been far from encouraging.'

"Currently, I am looking into what effort, if any, has been made to use VSA within the Department in order to ensure the experiences can be captured for future policy decisions in this area. In addition, I have initiated a DoD sponsored independent study by the University of Florida to assess the reliability of VSA. Dr. Humble and another VSA manufacturer are participating in this study due to be completed January 2006. The $500,000 that Dr. Humble stated might be available for VSA funding is probably related to a proposal by Dr. Humble to seek US Special Operations Command (SOCOM) funding to miniaturize a version of his laptop-sized system. SOCOM reviewed the proposal and ultimately declined to fund the initiative."

"We are seeking new technologies to replace or support the polygraph," the letter continued. "The Department has significantly increased its investment into the research of emerging credibility assessment technology by 60% over the last five years. Some highly advanced non-polygraph and non-voice technologies are showing tremendous statistical promise in the testing and evaluation phase. Our intent is to field the resulting assessment tools as soon as they can be scientifically validated."

Cambone closed his letter by thanking the senator for his interest and promising to deliver a CD containing a compilation of information and research data on voice stress technologies.

By writing "...we look to leverage only technologies with a firm scientific foundation," Cambone seemed to indicate confidence that neither the senator nor members of his staff would fact-check his statements or look at the documents he had cited.

Had Senator Santorum's people read the aforementioned 2002 NRC report, they would have found researchers had cited 57 research studies touted by the APA and concluded that the majority were "unreliable, unscientific and biased."

Furthermore, they would not have been surprised to learn that Dr. Ryan -- the man mentioned earlier in this book as a member of the Cambone team dispatched to GITMO in

October 2004 -- had served as liaison between NRC researchers and government polygraph officials involved in the NRC project.

Had the senator's staffers dug deeper into Cambone's claim that SOCOM officials had "reviewed the proposal and ultimately declined to fund the initiative," they would have learned Cambone wasn't telling the whole truth about that matter either.

In fact, according to NITV officials, they would have learned Cambone had, apparently working with Haave, pulled SOCOM's CVSA®-related research and development funding after it had already been approved by DACP.

Evidence of the DACP funding approval for FIST can be found in both a February 2005 DACP budget document[35] and in the issue of *Special Operations Technology Online*[36] published August 16, 2005 -- ten days before the date of Cambone's letter to Senator Santorum.

Had Senator Santorum's people dug deeper into what Cambone offered as the report's conclusion (i.e., that the research offered "little or no scientific basis for the use of the computer voice stress analyzer or similar voice measurement instruments"), they would have discovered two worthwhile recommendations near the end of the report.

On page 8, they would have found that researchers recommended "an expanded research effort directed at methods for detecting and deterring major security threats, including efforts to improve techniques for security screening."

On the following page, they would have found specific details about what researchers had written in their recommendations.

"A substantial portion of our recommended expanded research program should be administered by an organization or organizations with no operational responsibility for detecting deception and no institutional commitment to using or training practitioners of a particular technique," they wrote. "The research program should follow accepted standards for scientific research, use rules and procedures designed to eliminate biases that might influence the findings, and operate under normal rules of scientific freedom and openness to the extent possible while protecting national security."

Unfortunately, Senator Santorum's staffers didn't dig deep at all and appear to have accepted Cambone's information in no-questions-asked fashion. In doing so, they cleared the way for Cambone's "DoD sponsored independent study" to move forward in sunny Florida.

# CHAPTER THIRTEEN:
## 'The Florida Study'

A \$336,000 study[37] commissioned by Cambone in 2005 and paid for by CIFA, "Voice Stress Analyzer Instrumentation Evaluation" was published March 17, 2006, and yielded 66 pages of pro-polygraph results that came to be referred to as "The Florida Study."

Purporting to assess the reliability of CVSA® and another voice-focused technology known as Layered-Voice Analysis (LVA), The Florida Study was conducted by Harry Hollien and James D. Harnsberger, both Ph.D.-holding researchers at the University of Florida-Gainesville. Their overall conclusion: "neither the CVSA nor the LVA were sensitive to the presence of deception or stress."

Not everyone agreed with that conclusion.

In a letter dated June 14, 2006, and addressed to officials at NITV, Robert MacCaughelty, Ph.D., pointed out the flaws in the DoD-funded research.

"The study's elegance of design is both its apparent strength and ultimately its fatal flaw in doing what it set out to do," wrote Dr. MacCaughelty, a psychologist based in Charlotte, North Carolina. "The design has the appearance of good science; however, at deeper examination it is a transparent use of the Straw Man Fallacy in logic to bolster the position of disproving the efficacy of voice stress analysis and NITV protocols use in deception detection."

Dr. MacCaughelty went on to write that The Florida Study was set up to lead to the conclusion found. And he wasn't alone in criticizing the study.

A professor/research scientist at Georgia State University's J. Mack Robinson College conducted an "independent peer review" of the Hollien-Harnsberger effort. I was able to obtain a copy of a letter, dated February 11, 2009, in which he described the reviewers' findings.

He wrote that he "chose to proceed as if this effort were a typical panel of referees for a manuscript submitted to the Journal *Science*."

"Accordingly," he explained, "the manuscript was redacted of identifiers of the authors" -- including his own.

The professor went on to provide details about the "referees."

Three of the four held doctorate degrees and specialized in biosecurity and personnel reliability programs, decision science, and criminal and behavioral psychopathies, he explained. The fourth was a professional engineer who specializes in study design.

Their reviews included some scathing remarks.

"In conclusion, the claims of the paper are not supported," wrote Reviewer 1.

"The conclusions are not supported by the study," wrote Reviewer 2, noting disagreement between researchers about what should be measured, what was being measured and how the measurement should be done.

"There is no way that this manuscript, if presented for the very ordinary and normal peer review process for scientific publication, would pass even a perfunctory 'smell test,'" wrote Reviewer 3. "There's a fatally flawed approach to science that is best described as 'I wouldn't have seen it if I hadn't believed it.' This manuscript reeks of such presumption."

"The conclusions do seem supported by the data if taken at face value," concluded Reviewer 4. "Yet the conceptualization of the study, the description of the data, the experimental methods, and the analysis methodology all lack credibility. The overall conclusions therefore cannot be supported by the study as reported."

Joining Dr. MacCaughelty and the four independent reviewers in criticizing the study was Paul R. Hollrah, a man who has written extensively about the turf war.

Early in an article[38] that appeared September 6, 2006, on the web site of *The Conservative Voice* (now part of the popular conservative politics website, Townhall.com), Hollrah asked a pointed question.

"So what if someone were to tell you that a technology called Computer *[sic]* Voice Stress Analysis, CVSA, the most important new development in the science of truth verification, is being denied to intelligence specialists in Iraq, Afghanistan, Guantanamo, and elsewhere by policy directive from the Pentagon?"

He went on to provide details of the anti-CVSA® DoD policy decisions before using a passionate tone to end his article.

"In the global War on Terror, it is absolutely essential that we utilize every available weapon capable of subduing the enemy and saving the lives of Americans. To forego the deployment of a critical interrogation tool that is inexpensive, fast, effective, and user-friendly — for no better reason than to satisfy the whims and biases of one or two senior Pentagon bureaucrats — is unconscionable and irresponsible."

Within weeks of its publication, the article earned Hollrah a stern rebuke from Rob Andrews, a Deputy USD.

In a letter dated October 27, 2006, Andrews dismissed Hollrah's criticism of The Florida Study and leveled severe criticism in the opposite direction -- toward CVSA®.

"In 2005, the Department commissioned the University of Florida to conduct an independent scientific evaluation of CVSA," Andrews wrote. "The University's comprehensive research protocol included vendor involvement in procedures, training, and data evaluation. The study concluded that CVSA performed at 'chance levels.' That is, CVSA did not detect deception, truth, or the presence of stress any better than random guessing."

What Andrews did not explain, however, was that the only chance associated with the study appears to have been the "fat chance" CVSA® would get a fair shake.

In addition, he failed to mention some of the nitty-gritty details that might have called into question possible ethical issues, conflicts of interest and questionable activities related to the study.

More than three years later, a Washington, D.C.-based attorney requested a formal investigation into the award of a DoD contract to the University of Florida. I obtained a copy of the letter in which the attorney made the request on the condition that I promise to keep confidential both the name of the attorney and the name of the person who provided a copy of the letter.

In his letter, dated November 3, 2009, and addressed to officials at the offices of the DoD Inspector General, the Defense Criminal Investigative Service (DCIS) and the Government Accountability Office (GAO), the attorney detailed several factors that led him to request a formal inquiry.

"In 2005," he wrote, "members of Congress wanted to know why the U.S. Special Operations Command survey of the NITV's Computer Voice Stress Analyzer truth verification tool found it to be highly-accurate and reliable while, in contrast, the Department of Defense Polygraph Institute found its accuracy to be 'less than chance' in studies they funded, sponsored and/or conducted."

The attorney continued by pointing out how Congress had directed Cambone to order an independent study of CVSA® and how, in turn, a contract was awarded to the University of Florida.

Next, he lowered the boom and leveled accusations.

"Those in charge of this study failed to inform Congress that Dr. Hollien had conducted a questionable study of voice stress analysis (VSA) technology in 1986 and found its accuracy to be 'less than chance,'" he wrote.

"The Office of the USDI also failed to inform Congress that Dr. John Capps, brother of Michael Capps, a former director of DoDPI and at the time a high-ranking USDI employee, would supervise and oversee the study on behalf of the USDI.

"Although the guidelines for the study required it to be conducted utilizing mandatory protocols provided by the manufacturer," the letter continued, "Dr. Hollien, with the consent of the USDI and Dr. John Capps, simply ignored this prerequisite and used the protocols he employed in the 1985 study to discredit VSA technology.

"With the knowledge and consent of the USDI, Dr. Hollien replicated his earlier study – the outcome of which was predetermined. In the process, taxpayer's dollars were wasted, fraud was perpetrated, academic and government ethics were violated, and all concerned DoD-parties perpetrated highly questionable intelligence activities to protect the status quo."

The attorney concluded his letter with some high-voltage claims.

"Further, Dr. Hollien also ignored the manufacturer's protests, and even applied high-voltage electric shocks to human test subjects during the course of his DoD-funded CVSA research.

"Predictably, the results of the study replicated those of Dr. Hollien's previous study, and concluded the CVSA's accuracy was 'less than chance,' despite existing classified evidence held by the DoD to the contrary. The USDI simply suppressed the classified evidence of the CVSA's accuracy and released the flawed results of Dr. Hollien's study.

"An investigation into this matter is clearly warranted. The information provided above indicates these events were intentionally fraudulent and an abuse of taxpayer dollars. The above is in addition to the millions of taxpayer dollars that DoDPI (now referred to as the Defense Academy for Credibility Assessment — DACA) has spent on similar fraudulent 'studies' of VSA. Investigations of such matters are critical to expose fraud and bring those responsible to justice."

Sadly, I could find no evidence the attorney's letter resulted in any sort of federal investigation(s). I did, however, find evidence that another kind of investigation had taken place soon after The Florida Study's findings were released.

# CHAPTER FOURTEEN:
# 'Innocent Until Proven Guilty'

Less than two weeks after The Florida Study was released, ABC News aired a stinging segment, "Innocent Until Proven Guilty,"[39] during the March 30, 2006, edition of the network's magazine-style program, *Primetime*. Playing a leading role in the segment was the network's chief investigative reporter, Brian Ross.

Though Ross did not mention The Florida Study by name, he cited its findings early and often during the seven-minute report. He was assisted in the effort by *Primetime* host Chris Cuomo who introduced the piece by raising and lowering his voice for dramatic effect.

"We're about to take you somewhere with a lofty-, even futuristic-sounding name," he said, "the National Institute for Truth Verification.

"It's run by Dr. Charles Humble, who has become a wealthy man by selling what he says is a virtually-foolproof system to help catch criminals and liars -- not by what they say, but how they say it.

"But some critics say his invention is no better than a sewing machine for determining the truth," Cuomo continued. Then he introduced Ross.

With "Voice Lie Detector?" superimposed on the lower-left corner of the screen, the segment began with video showing Humble seated before a laptop computer and speaking into a microphone as the voice of the reporter described what viewers were seeing on their television screens.

"This is Dr. Charles Humble's truth-verification system -- a laptop, equipped with a microphone and loaded with a software program called 'the Computer Voice Stress Analyzer' -- The C-V-S-A. It captures a kind of voice print said to detect stress and, therefore, deception."

The scene shifted to a typical interview set up, with Ross sitting across from Humble in a well-lit South Florida hotel room as Humble described how his technology works, apparently in response to a question from the reporter.

Humble concluded his remarks by saying, "We have a remarkable record of success with the system."

"This has become the 'gold standard'?" Ross asked.

"That's correct," Humble replied.

The on-screen image shifted to B-roll footage of law enforcement officers sitting in front of laptop computers in a classroom setting, learning about CVSA®. The reporter's voice accompanied the footage.

"But it has become the gold standard, being sold to more and more police departments every week, despite growing questions about the scientific validity of the machine and about the credentials of Dr. Humble himself."

The scene shifted back to the one-on-one interview setting with Ross asking Humble another question.

"Is there a single scientific study that shows that this actually works?"

"I don't believe that there has been an independent scientific study that shows this actually works," Humble replied, his face filling the screen in an extreme close-up.

Keyword: independent.

"Not one?" asked Ross, shown waving one finger in front of him, left to right.

"I don't believe there has been," Humble confirmed, again in close-up.

Again, the scene changed and viewers were shown video footage, shot by a camera mounted atop a wall inside a sparsely-furnished room. A young man could be seen seated on a bench against a wall on the opposite side of the room. The reporter's voice returned.

"Dr. Humble says the machine can only really be tested in the field where he says it has an accuracy rate of 98 percent."

At this point, it would have made sense for Ross to speak with CVSA® end users like the ones I interviewed; instead, he took the interview in the opposite direction.

Without warning, the distressed voice of the young man shown on screen could be heard -- "I didn't do it, I swear to God" -- while his words were superimposed on the screen. Then the reporter's voice returned.

"But he clearly was not including what happened in the case of 14-year-old Michael Crow, the California boy who confessed to killing his sister," Ross continued in voiceover mode. "The machine got it very wrong."

Quickly, the head-and-shoulders image of a young girl appeared on the screen and the camera slowly pushed in until the girl's face was filling the screen, accompanied by the reporter's voice.

"Twelve-year-old Stephanie Crow was found stabbed to death in her bedroom," Ross explained as the on-screen image changed to show the outside of a police station. "Michael was brought into the Escondido Police Department for questioning and hooked up to the CVSA in the middle of the night."

The scene returned to the interrogation room where an exchange took place between a police detective and the young man. The words of each appeared, superimposed on the screen.

"Is today Thursday?" the detective asked.

"Yes," Michael answered.

"Did you take Stephanie's life?"

"No."

The reporter's voice returned, informing viewers that the detective was telling Michael about the results of the CVSA® exam.

"And it showed that you had some deception on some of the questions," the detective could be heard saying.

The scene shifted to a full-frame image of Michael's face years later as he described his thoughts about this episode in his life.

"I started to think that maybe the machine's right," Michael said, "especially when they added on top of it that the machine was getting my subconscious feelings on it, that I could be lying and not even know it."

The reporter's voice returned to accompany video imagery of Michael inside the interrogation room, sobbing.

"Once he was told he had failed the test, Michael says he began to doubt his own memory and wonder whether maybe he had killed his sister."

Michael's face appeared in close-up again.

"I didn't want to go to prison, and I just wanted to be out of that room," he said, "so my only option was to say, 'Yeah, I guess I did it,' and then hope for the best."

More interrogation-room imagery appeared and viewers were able to hear and read Michael's confession as the halfway point of the video neared.

"I got a knife, went into her room and then I stabbed her," he said.

Next, the scene shifted to courtroom footage showing a longhaired man with a walrus-style mustache as Ross chimed in again.

"Just one week before the trial was to begin, police found DNA evidence that lead to the real killer, a transient who is now in prison for killing Michael's sister."

The scene changed again, this time showing the image of a CVSA®-marked laptop with the words, "NATIONAL INSTITUTE FOR TRUTH VERIFICATION," in all capital letters, printed on a piece of paper placed strategically nearby. Ross began to use his words like a scalpel.

"The false confession and Dr. Humble's machine denounced by the judge," he said.

The scene shifted to show Humble in what was described as a promotional video. Ross added to the imagery by injecting more words critical of Humble and his technology.

"But there's no mention of the Michael Crow case or of any problem on the promotional videos Dr. Humble uses to sell his machines to American law enforcement. And, throughout the materials, Humble is always introduced as 'Doctor Humble' even though, as *Primetime* discovered, he is not a medical doctor and has not earned a Ph.D. degree from an accredited university."

After a quick cut, the scene returned to the hotel room-interview setting where another exchange took place between the reporter and Humble. Much to the reporter's delight, it appeared, his interview subject did not wilt into a puddle of guilt upon hearing the reporter's questions.

"Do you feel comfortable calling yourself 'Doctor Humble'?" Ross asked.

"Yes," Humble replied.

"You do?"

"Yes."

The reporter's voice could be heard again as the scene shifted to show the walls inside Humble's office, a framed document and finally the outside of a shopping center.

"The Ph.D. diploma he has on his office wall -- doctor of psychology -- was awarded by a Bible college in Indiana that used to be in this strip mall where Humble's first office was located."

The scene shifted back to the one-on-one interview as Humble provided the name of the school that conferred his sheepskin.

"Indiana Christian University."

"Is that an accredited university?" Ross asked.

"No. It's not accredited," Humble replied briefly.

Before he could offer further explanation, Ross interrupted him.

"And you call yourself 'Dr. Humble' based on that?"

Humble replied affirmatively, prompting yet another question from Ross.

"Is that honest, do you think?"

"I think it is," Humble replied.

"So this Bible school awarded you a Ph.D in psychology?" Ross continued.

"An honorary, yes," Humble answered.

Despite the fact that classwork has never been required of those upon whom honorary degrees are conferred, Ross went on to ask Humble if he had taken any classes at the school and, if so, to describe them. Humble explained that he had taken six hours of Bible classes, and the interview portion of the broadcast ended.

Did the personal attack on Humble's academic credentials prove anything? Yes. He's not perfect. Not as a human being or as a spokesperson for CVSA®. Though those facts have had no impact on the effectiveness of Humble's technology, Ross pressed on as if they did, and the scene shifted back to the studio where Cuomo and Ross picked Humble to pieces.

"You should have hooked him up to his own machine, but tell me seriously, why is he doing so well?" Cuomo asked Ross.

"Well, this machine, according to people who study it, really works as a kind of a prop," the reporter explained. "People who are guilty and think the machine works are inclined to tell the truth because they think the machine will work. But it has the problem of also getting people who are not guilty to somehow think they have to confess. Perhaps they've repressed it. Recent studies showed you'd be just as well off flipping a coin; it's that accurate or lack of accuracy."

"And, adding to the problem here," Cuomo interjected, "is that this isn't something that's used in one or two places. This has now become used even by the higher-ups."

"Fifteen-hundred American police departments, according to 'Dr. Humble,' as well, which we found, he's now selling it -- or has been selling it -- to the U.S. military. They've used it in Guantanamo Bay, in Iraq and Afghanistan to interrogate important terror suspects, including Tariq Aziz, the former deputy prime minister (of Iraq).

"They have cleared eight or nine people in Iraq who are suspected of being terrorists," Ross replied. "They let them go based on this machine." *NOTE: According to NITV officials close to the CVSA® examiners -- including "Ed," the man mentioned earlier in this book -- who conducted the exams in question, the statement by Ross was simply not true. Instead, decisions to release individuals were based on both a lack of evidence and results of the CVSA® exams.*

"The Pentagon has done a study, and it now has banned its use," Ross continued. "They will not allow the military to use it because of their concern about its reliability."

"So what do you think the future is for Dr. Humble? What's gonna go on here?" Cuomo continued, feeding the reporter.

"Well, if the police departments think it works even if there's no scientific reliability, I guess they can buy it," Ross said. "It's a very expensive prop though at $10,000 a piece."

"And give me a little sense of process," Cuomo said. "After that interview, when you gave him the Brian Ross special, what was his reaction?"

"Ahh, I don't think he was that pleased with the way the interview went," Ross said, feigning humility. "He has told us as much. He kept wondering how he did, and I assured him he did fine.

"He certainly told his story. I'd say he's a good salesman. He does a good job of selling this machine, but the fact that he has this degree of questionable background and a machine that has no real scientific basis. I think the fact that it is now becoming public may well be a problem for him."

Ending the segment, Cuomo stroked his reporter's ego.

"Unbeknownst to him, he was sitting down with ABC's number one truth-detector machine."

Ross had conveyed to television viewers two clear messages: Humble is a huckster; and his company's product, CVSA®, is some sort of modern-day technological "snake oil"). And he didn't stop there.

\* \* \*

In a print version[40] of "Innocent Until Proven Guilty?" that was available to visitors of the ABC News website at the time of this book's publication, Ross and three contributors -- Vic Walter, Joe Rhee and Avni Patel -- offered readers even more material under Ross' byline.

Ross began by informing readers about the "Pentagon study obtained by ABC News" and how researchers found that a new kind of voice lie detector used by the U.S. military and American police departments is no better than "flipping a coin" in detecting lies.

Next, Ross noted that the Pentagon had ordered a halt to its use but did not offer any specifics about the "order" which, I learned, was The Cambone Memo mentioned in an earlier chapter.

A description of the CVSA® set up (i.e., a laptop, microphone and software program) followed, accompanied by statements in which Ross described CVSA® as a "lie detector" Humble said is "foolproof."

Ross went on to rehash the fact that police departments nationwide rely on CVSA®, then quoted Humble as saying, "We have a remarkable record of success."

Under the subhead, "Confesses to Murder Based on Machine," Ross used nine paragraphs to highlight details of the Stephanie Crowe murder case in a manner that paralleled the television version sans video.

Under the next subhead, "Nothing More Than a Prop," Ross noted that: (1) the alleged murderer was later found innocent by virtue of the fact that DNA led to the arrest of another man; (2) an out-of-court settlement had been reached between NITV and the original suspect's family; and that (3) an NITV executive had "admitted under oath that the machine is not capable of detecting truth or lies."

Regarding those points, NITV officials are quick to point out that people outside of their purview were involved in the investigation in question and did not follow proper procedure for using CVSA®.

In addition, they said NITV wasn't the first and won't be the last company to decide, in agreement with its insurance company, to opt for an out-of-court settlement in lieu of spending inordinate amounts of time and money in litigation.

Finally, NITV officials are adamant when they say CVSA® technology detects real-world stress indicative of deception, not lies.

The article continued with the remaining paragraphs devoted to CVSA®-focused opinions of two less-than-unbiased "experts."

The first, John Palmatier, holds a Ph.D. in psychology and runs a polygraph examination business[41] in Florida. He was quoted as saying "(CVSA) is nothing more than a prop" and explaining that his own study found no scientific basis for claims made by Humble.[42]

Later, he was quoted as saying, "You could not accurately discriminate between truthful and deceptive subjects using that device."

In addition, he answered a Ross question about whether CVSA® could be used as a scare tactic by saying police officers have used it that way for years.

To his credit, Ross did include a quote from Humble in which the NITV founder made clear his stance about the technology being one investigative tool instead of an end-all solution for law officers. That, however, was about as friendly as the reporter would get.

Next, Ross brushed over a 1997 federal court case in Las Vegas that involved the arrest of a man, Vincent John Sedgwick, on an allegation he had served as a "lookout" for another person as that person raped a woman.

Though Ross painted a picture of the charges being based almost entirely on the outcome of a CVSA® exam, reality turned out to be far different.

After a judge dismissed the criminal case against Sedgwick for lack of evidence, Sedgwick's attorney, Ian Christopherson, began a new legal fight.

In the May 1999 edition of the American Bar Association's *ABA Journal*[43], Christopherson was cited as saying he intended to put the CVSA® -- as well as those who administered it to his client -- on trial. And he did.

Claiming the Henderson Police Department had falsely accused his client of being involved in a rape following a CVSA® examination, Sedgwick's lawyer filed a lawsuit in which he sought a seven-figure judgment against Humble, NITV, the city of Henderson, Nevada, its police chief, and two of the department's CVSA® examiners.

In the same article, Frank Horvath was quoted as saying, "Police seem to like (CVSA) because it produces the occasional confession, which saves them a lot of time and legwork," and was identified only as "a Michigan State University criminology professor who has studied lie detector technology for more than 30 years."

In the paragraphs that followed, Horvath was quoted two more times, but never identified as a man who, during the 1991-92 term, served as APA president. Perhaps the reporter didn't know.

Beyond that, the lawsuit story became more interesting.

"When the suit was filed," Humble wrote in his company's 2000/2001 newsletter distributed to CVSA® examiners, "the polygraph community, including most state polygraph associations, sent out letters to virtually every law enforcement agency describing the lawsuit as a result of utilizing an instrument that is not recognized as reliable.

"The intent of their letters was very clear, to 'scare' law enforcement away from purchasing or using the CVSA. As this case progressed, it became clear that this individual did not file this case on his own, but rather with both the encouragement and backing of the polygraph community (which he admitted to a reporter).

"In other words," Humble continued, "this case was filed against (me) and NITV in order to achieve what the polygraph community was unable to accomplish in the marketplace. Their goal was simple, to deal the CVSA a critical blow and stop what has now become a stampede to switch from the polygraph to CVSA. It became obvious to the polygraph community that they had lost the battle for the law enforcement community in the marketplace and so they resorted to a federal lawsuit using Mr. Sedgwick as their vehicle to, they hoped, fatally damage the CVSA.

"Not only did they not accomplish their goal, but after one year of hearing evidence, on May 25, 1999, United States District Court Judge Philip Pro dismissed their suit in a summary judgment statement stating that they had failed to prove even one allegation of the suit."

In an attempt to verify Humble's claims, I tried to locate copies of news articles about the case that might have appeared in one of three Las Vegas area newspapers. Unfortunately, Henderson's only newspaper at the time of the controversy no longer exists, and the archives of two other publications -- the *Las Vegas Sun* and *Las Vegas Courier-Journal* -- yielded no results. I did, however, obtain a copy of a ruling on the case from the U.S. Court of Appeals for the Ninth District.

Dated January 17, 2001, and based upon an appeal argued and submitted before the court November 17, 2000, the ruling included this key line: "Because Sedgwick has not shown that the results of the CVSA damaged him in any way, his arguments fail."

After milking the lawsuit topic for all it was worth, the focus of ABC News' article shifted to Humble's credentials -- a rehash of the television report -- and then to the use of CVSA® by the Pentagon.

Next, Ross mentioned that military officials had confirmed to him that CVSA® had been used in prisons at Guantanamo Bay and in Iraq before being banned for use within DoD. And it had.

From there, he moved on to a second "expert," Robert Rogalski. Like Haave, he was a senior DoD official at the time of his interview with Ross.

According to the article, Rogalski told Ross that an exhaustive Pentagon-ordered study of CVSA® had found little or no relationship between the machine's reading and the actual presence or absence of deception and stress. One paragraph later, Rogalski compared CVSA®'s reliability to that of flipping a coin.

Were they talking about The Florida Study? It seemed as if they were, but both seemed to know better than to mention it by name, warts and all.

Ross continued to "push the envelope" when he added that Rogalski was alarmed to hear about a document from NITV in which company officials bragged that one of their employees had used the machine in Baghdad to free a number of individuals, including some who were terror suspects and others who had been accused of crimes without any evidence being presented.

"It's very troubling. How truthful was that result, and if there's a question, then I'm concerned about that," Rogalski said before adding he is especially concerned about the prospect that some of those suspected terrorists were actual terrorists."

\* \* \*

Should anyone be surprised by Ross' unbalanced reports? Hardly. His track record includes many instances of getting things wrong.

Writing for Salon.com, Glenn Greenwald devoted much time and attention to coverage of news reports by Ross about an alleged link between post-9/11 Anthrax attacks in the United States and Iraq.

At one of the most critical times in American history, the weeks following the 9/11 and anthrax attacks, Greenwald wrote in an April 2007 article [44], ABC News and Brian Ross published multiple, highly inflammatory reports, aggressively linking Iraq to the anthrax attacks, which turned out to be completely false.

146

More recently, ABC News had to issue an apology in an update to a July 20, 2012, report in which Ross wrongly identified Colorado Tea Party member Jim Holmes as the shooter who had killed 12 people and wounded 58 others at an Aurora, Colorado, movie theater.[45]

Should Ross ever decide to do a follow-up story to balance out his hit piece on Humble and CVSA®, I recommend he follow a few easy paths leading to accurate information.

First, he should conduct a simple online search of the phrase "polygraph lawsuit." Doing so will reveal scores of startling examples of polygraph flaws that have surfaced both inside and outside of courtrooms across America.

He should also contact officials at The Innocence Project for news about some of the well-publicized polygraph failures they've encountered. The case of Jeff Deskovic stands as a prime example.

According to a case profile[46] on the organization's website, Deskovic spent 16 years behind bars after being convicted in January 1991 of a murder he did not commit. Though three polygraph exams and related questions led to an alleged confession, DNA evidence eventually cleared him of the charges.

Finally, Ross should look into the backgrounds of some of the nation's top polygraph loyalists. Two, in particular, come to mind.

A self-described polygraph expert who once served as president of the APA (1978-79), Edward I. Gelb is the principal behind Los Angeles-based Intercept Inc., a company licensed by the state of California to perform private investigation work.

During a career spanning more than three decades, Gelb has been involved in many high-profile criminal investigations in which polygraph examinations played a role. Among his most-highly-publicized cases was the investigation into the December 1996 murder of JonBenet Ramsey in Boulder, Colorado.

On May 30, 2000, for instance, Gelb discussed the Ramsey case as a guest of Geraldo Rivera on CNN's *Geraldo Rivera Live*.[47]. Six days later, he appeared on CNN's *Newsstand*[48] with Greta Van Susteren.

The hosts of both programs introduced Gelb as a "polygraph expert" and asked him to confirm that he had conducted "more 30,000 polygraph exams" since 1969.

Gelb offered affirmative replies and, in so doing, confirmed he had conducted more than 700 exams per year -- or two per day, seven days per week -- for 42 years.

Compare those numbers to the generally-recognized standard that polygraphers can be expected to complete only two exams per day and, unless my math is off, there seems to be a disconnect.

Gelb also expressed confidence in the accuracy of his exams and attached two figures -- 94 and 95 percent -- to his remarks. Polygraph accuracy figures that high have never been verified by any objective scientific research.

Perhaps most damning about Gelb is a bit of information -- "Dr. Edward Gelb, Ph.D." -- that appeared on his company's website, http://PolygraphExpert.com, until early January 2013, when, inexplicably, the site was down.

Unlike Humble, who was awarded his honorary doctorate by a legitimate, albeit unaccredited, institution of higher education, Gelb began calling himself "doctor," according to the George Maschke at http://AntiPolygraph.org[49], after purchasing a doctorate degree from LaSalle University -- not to be confused with the reputable university of the same name in Philadelphia.

Located in Mandeville, Louisiana, this LaSalle was described as a "diploma mill" and shut down by the FBI in 1996.[50]

Not wanting to rely solely upon that claim, I attempted to contact Gelb three times between February 27, 2012, and June 21, 2012, using the email address (i.e., egelb43972@aol.com) that appeared below his photo on his company website. In short, I wanted to know whether or not he had purchased a phony LaSalle degree.

Gelb never replied to my messages.

Several attempts to reach him by phone since March 7, 2012, have failed as well. Each time I called, the person answering his office phone told me he was unavailable and took my contact information.

During the most recent call, which took place August 30, 2012, a female -- who said she was a "temp" -- answered my call. After she gave me the same response I had received earlier, I asked her to do me a favor and simply confirm that the email address I had been using in my attempts to reach Gelb *was* correct. She told me it was.

If, indeed, Gelb earned a doctorate legitimately, why is he so reluctant to go on record to acknowledge such?

The second polygraph loyalist Ross should interview is Porco.

At the time this book went to press, Porco was serving as DoD's Deputy Director for Counterintelligence Services, the senior DoD policy official on matters related to the polygraph and one of the nation's highest-ranking counterintelligence officials.

Despite the fact that 15 federal government agencies, according to a January 2013 McClatchy News report[51], combine to use the polygraph to screen more than 70,000 job applicants and employees annually, national security leaks continue to occur on a frequent and regular basis.

In his position inside DoD, Porco was certainly expected to play a key role in DNI Clapper Jr.'s effort[52] announced June 25, 2012, to stop leaks from within federal government agencies via beefed-up polygraph exams.

While conducting research for this book August 2, 2012, I came across something involving Porco that was both astonishing and disturbing: he was using his federal government position to bolster his credibility as a private investigator and, one must assume, as a means to increase business and revenues for his private company, Porco Investigative Services of National Harbor, Maryland.

On the "Career Highlights" page[53] of his company's website, the "Counterintelligence" tab featured a description of Porco's aforementioned high-level position of employment with DoD: *...with responsibility for policy development and oversight for the DoD Polygraph/Credibility Assessment, and Technical Surveillance Countermeasures.*

This was, of course, a disturbing discovery as our nation's top intelligence officials were in the midst of grappling with serious concerns about national security leaks.

Highlighted in articles that appeared in the *National Post*[54], *The New York Times*[55], *The Weekly Standard*[56], and other news outlets in early August 2012, those concerns had prompted DNI Clapper to call for expanded use of the polygraph as a tool to combat the leaks.

Immediately upon seeing this information displayed so publicly, I fired off an email to Lieutenant Colonel James Gregory, a DoD public affairs officer. I asked the colonel to confirm whether or not the individual who appeared to be the proprietor of the business was, indeed, the high-level DoD employee described on the website. In addition, I told the colonel I would have a follow-up question for him if he were able to provide that confirmation.

Less than 24 hours later, I received confirmation from Colonel Gregory and replied with a follow-up question.

"I found it unusual that a person in the counter intel biz would advertise his arguably-sensitive position on a private investigations business website," I wrote. "Isn't there a policy or regulation that prohibits that?"

Another 24 hours passed before I received his reply via email.

"Bob — There is no specific policy regarding the security aspects of posting his position, however there is a policy related to implied endorsement of his company by posting it," Colonel Gregory wrote. "Thanks for bringing this to our attention; Mr. Porco has been informed and is taking the appropriate steps to bring his website into compliance. Best, LTC Gregory"

Less than 24 hours after receiving Colonel Gregory's message, the page in question on Porco's company website had been scrubbed of the questionable content.

This wasn't, however, Porco's first "rodeo." He had played a key role in another recent scandal involving the agency's polygraph program.

I came across evidence of that scandal while reading The Polygraph Files[57], a series of articles by Marisa Taylor, a McClatchy News investigative reporter.

In one[58] of Taylor's articles, Porco was highlighted as a key player involved in crafting DoD's official response to allegations of abusive polygraph techniques being used by officials at the National Reconnaissance Office (NRO).

Though I never served in counterintelligence, I did possess a security clearance while serving as an Air Force officer and think I have a pretty good feel for what constitute a conflict of interest, a breach of ethics and/or an implied endorsement. That said, I remain stunned someone so high up in the DoD "food chain" would do something like this — or even have time to be moonlighting outside of his high-stakes Pentagon position.

Wondering whether my reaction was appropriate or "over the top," I contacted a retired counterintelligence operative with whom I've been friends for several years and asked him for his thoughts.

"Even privates in the Army know such actions go against DoD ethics and conflict of interest directives," he said, agreeing to speak with me only on the promise of anonymity. "It shows me how much the standards have dropped.

"In the old days, someone in such a high-level (counterintelligence) position would never even think about owning a PI business, never mind advertising on the internet *AND* showing his current government position to bolster his image."

# CHAPTER FIFTEEN:
# Spies, Lies, and Skeptics

Though ABC News' Ross avoided mentioning it in his piece about CVSA®, one thing remains true: when it comes to controversy, the polygraph attracts it like a magnet attracts iron filings. Examples are everywhere.

Conduct your own research on the topic of convicted spies, and you'll find the names of John Anthony Walker Jr., Jonathan Jay Pollard, Ana Belen Montes, and other U.S. government employees. Moreover, you'll find many of the folks convicted of spying for foreign governments had been subject to regular polygraph examinations as a condition of their federal government employment. One must assume they were able to beat those exams -- some for years and years before being caught!

How did they do it? Myriad techniques exist via which people claim they can beat the polygraph. And, for those unfamiliar with those techniques, a virtual cottage industry of experts -- online and offline -- stands willing to assist others in trying to "beat the polygraph" or otherwise prove it an unreliable means for detecting lies.

The list of techniques includes, but is not limited to, the following: 1) Learning in advance how to manipulate your body's blood pressure and heart rate and apply your skills while taking the test; 2) Placing a sharp object (i.e., a nail or tack) in your shoe and causing yourself pain while answering questions; 3) Biting the side of your tongue before answering questions; and 4) Contracting your anal sphincter muscle while answering questions.

Unlike those parlaying polygraph testing into income streams (i.e., Gelb, Palmatier, Porco et al), a number of high-ranking government officials have, through their actions, signaled their agreement with polygraph skeptics.

In an article[59] published December 20, 1985, in the *Los Angeles Times*, Norman Kempster reported that George Schulz, then serving as President Ronald Reagan's Secretary of State, was not a fan of the polygraph and, in fact, had threatened to resign rather than submit to a polygraph examination.

Former CIA Director R. James Woolsey seemed to harbor the same sentiment, some of which appeared in a Ronald Kessler article, "Spies, Lies, Averted Eyes,"[60] published in the March 8, 1994, edition of *The New York Times*. An excerpt of that article appears below:

The day after the arrest of the accused spy Aldrich H. Ames was announced, the Director of Central Intelligence, R. James Woolsey, met with several hundred C.I.A. employees in the agency's auditorium at Langley, Virginia. After recounting what employees already knew from the news media, Mr. Woolsey -- whose address was seen on closed-circuit television by every C.I.A. employee -- spent five minutes explaining why he himself had refused to take a polygraph test, as other recent directors had done. Besides the fact that political appointees are not required to take such tests, Mr. Woolsey said he remained "skeptical" about the polygraph's effectiveness.

Another CIA director, John Deutch, famously made the news the following year for taking a stand similar to Shultz and Woolsey.

New at the agency, Deutch was quoted by reporter Tim Weiner in a *New York Times* article[61] December 10, 1995, as saying the CIA's "reliance on the polygraph is truly insane."

Almost two years later, a man who quite possibly ranks as the "Mother of All Polygraph Skeptics" testified before the U.S. Senate Committee on the Judiciary Subcommittee on Administrative Oversight and the Courts on the topic of the polygraph.

With his occasional use of boldface type preserved, below is an excerpt from the transcript of the September 29, 1997, testimony of Dr. Drew Campbell Richardson, an FBI supervisory special agent assigned to the bureau's Laboratory Division:

"With regard to polygraph screening, I submit the following to you:

"1. *It is completely without any theoretical foundation and has absolutely no validity.* Although there is disagreement amongst scientists about the use of polygraph testing in criminal matters, there is almost universal agreement that polygraph screening is completely invalid and should be stopped. As one of my colleagues frequently says, the diagnostic value of this type of testing is no more than that of astrology or tea-leaf reading.

"2. If this test had any validity (which it does not), both my own experience, and published scientific research has proven, that **anyone can be taught to beat this type of polygraph exam in a few minutes.**

"3. Because of the nature of this type of examination, it would normally be expected to produce large numbers of false positive results (falsely accusing an examinee of lying about some issue). As a result of the great consequences of doing this with large numbers of law enforcement and intelligence community officers, the test has now been manipulated to reduce false positive results, but consequently has no power to detect deception in espionage and other national security matters. Thus, *I believe that there is virtually no probability of catching a spy with the use of polygraph screening techniques.* I think a careful examination of the Aldrich Ames case will reveal that any shortcomings in the use of the polygraph were *not* simply errors on the part of the polygraph examiners involved, and would not have been eliminated if FBI instead of CIA polygraphers had conducted these examinations. Instead I believe this is largely a reflection of the complete lack of validity of this methodology. *To the extent that we place any confidence in the results of polygraph screening, and as a consequence shortchange traditional security vetting techniques, I think our national security is severely jeopardized.*

"4. Because of the theoretical considerations involving false positive results and because of anecdotal stories told to me by self-alleged victims of polygraph screening, *I believe that the Bureau is routinely falsely accusing job applicants of drug usage or drug dealing.* Not only is this result irreparably harming these individuals, but it is likely denying the Bureau access to qualified and capable employees. Although these individuals do not have an inalienable right to Federal Government employment, they do have an inalienable right to just treatment by their government.

"5. I believe that claims of cost effectiveness, and the utility of polygraph screening are altogether wrong, reflect misplaced priorities, and lead to activities that are damaging to individuals and this country.

156

"I think the aforementioned problems with polygraph continue to exist within the Bureau and elsewhere for the following reasons:

"1.     Polygraph research (direction, funding, and evaluation), training, and operational review is controlled by those who practice polygraphy and depend upon it for a living. This is tantamount to having the government's cancer research efforts controlled by the tobacco industry. Independent scientific experts must be (and have not been) consulted to obtain an objective view of polygraphy.

"2.    Within the Bureau, polygraph examiners who have little or no understanding of the scientific principles underlying their practice, report to mid-level managers who are largely ignorant of polygraph matters. These in turn report to executives, who have real problems for which they seek needed solutions (e.g., the need to protect national security from the danger of espionage, and the need to hire employees with appropriate backgrounds). These executives are left unable to evaluate that polygraph is not a viable solution and do not comprehend that ignorance and mis-information are built into their own command structure.

"3. The fact that the human physiology is marvelously wonderful and complex, that polygraph methods have been able to accurately record this physiology for most of this century and beyond, and the fact that computerized acquisition and evaluation of this data is now available, in no way compensates for the vast shortcomings of polygraph applications and questioning formats. State of the art technology utilized on faulty applications amounts to nothing more than garbage in, garbage out.

"In conclusion and because of all these considerations, I would recommend that the Bureau administratively abandon polygraph screening, support meaningful research related to criminal-specific testing, and would call upon this body, either through immediate legislation or through further hearings dealing specifically with polygraph matters, to begin the process of producing A Comprehensive Polygraph Protection Act. Such an act could protect employees and applicants for Federal jobs from the abuses that this Senate has previously protected other Americans from."

In addition to a former Secretary of State, two former CIA directors and an FBI expert, two federal judges have weighed in on the polygraph controversy in their own unique ways.

U.S. Supreme Court Associate Justice Clarence Thomas appeared to qualify himself as a polygraph skeptic when he wrote about the technology in the Supreme Court's majority opinion[62] of the 1998 case, *U.S. v. Scheffer*.

"To this day," he wrote, "the scientific community remains extremely polarized about the reliability of polygraph techniques. [T]here is simply no way to know in a particular case whether a polygraph examiner's conclusion is accurate, because certain doubts and uncertainties plague even the best polygraph exams."

Conversely, on October 1, 2009, federal Judge Norman Mordue of the Northern District Court of New York ruled in *Gjurovich v. United States* that the results of CVSA® examinations were admissible in his court for use in determining whether a convicted sex offender is telling the truth about his activities. Such a ruling set a pretty weighty precedent for polygraph loyalists to match.

With numerous high-ranking federal government officials -- *including judges* -- siding against the polygraph and/or with CVSA®, one might think others would have second thoughts about the technology as well. Keyword: might.

# CHAPTER SIXTEEN:
## The 'Birth' of PCASS

"We interrupt this broadcast with a special news bulletin!"

Though it wasn't quite as blatant as a news bulletin interrupting primetime television programming, a pre-solicitation notice for PCASS appeared at the Federal Business Opportunities website[63] April 10, 2006 -- only ten days after ABC News aired its hit piece on CVSA®.

"The Department of Defense Polygraph Institute is anticipating sole source award to Lafayette Instrument Company for digitized question presentation capability for Portable Credibility Assessment Screening Systems (PCASS)," began solicitation number H9CI0160091. "This technology was developed by the Lafayette Instrument Company.

"The Portable Credibility Assessment Screening System (PCASS) is a hand-held system, much like a personal digital assistant (PDA), that is used for rapid real-time credibility assessment of an individual being questioned," the notice continued, ending with contact information for officials at the Defense Information Systems Agency, Procurement and Logistics (a.k.a., "DITCO-Scott"), at Scott Air Force Base, Illinois, just east of Saint Louis, Missouri.

Curiously, the notice made no mention of the involvement of researchers at Johns Hopkins University in Baltimore despite the fact that, according to a report[64] published in November 2006, researchers at the distinguished research institution's Applied Physics Laboratory developed the decision algorithm (Version 2.1) that integrates electrodermal and vasomotor responses time-locked with stimulus presentation in order to make a decision.

Wanting to learn more about the contracts via which PCASS was "born," I filed several FOIA requests during the summer of 2012 with DIA/DITCO, the agency at Scott Air Force Base, Illinois, that handles PCASS-related contracting matters.

I began by asking for copies of any and all PCASS-related contracts awarded to Lafayette Instrument since the inception of the program in 2006. Though I did not receive all of the documents requested, I learned a lot from the ones I did receive.

For instance, I learned that "Preliminary" had, without explanation, replaced "Portable" in the official name of the device appearing in orders placed in April 2007[65] and June 2008[66].

Why the change? Perhaps its developers realized they needed to include a caveat (i.e., the word "preliminary") in the official name of the device as a means to soften criticism they undoubtedly knew they would encounter in the near future.

I learned that early descriptions of PCASS showed the devices yielded only "red light (i.e., deception indicated)" or "green light (i.e., "no deception indicated") decisions while later descriptions included "yellow light" capabilities.

Was that due to a change in the algorithm being used? I wanted to know.

In addition, I learned early PCASS contracts called for the inclusion of wireless headsets while later contracts did not. Why the change?

On July 6, 2012, I began posing questions to officials at DITCO-Scott and DIA about the birth and development of PCASS.

I asked who, exactly, came up with the idea to develop PCASS, upon what need(s) the development was based, and if a "needs assessment" was ever conducted to justify the development. Of course, I asked for details, too.

I asked questions about when the PCASS project began and who was involved as well as about the delivery of the first prototype and the date when DoD placed its first order with Lafayette Instrument.

Beyond those questions, I asked several more aimed at learning more about the process via which the project got off the ground (i.e., "Whose idea was it?") and how Lafayette Instrument was awarded the PCASS contract. Those questions included phrases like "open solicitation," "sole-source contract," and "only contractor capable."

I asked about changes and/or improvements made to PCASS since its birth and for explanations of what prompted them.

I asked for an explanation of why and when the spelled-out version of the name for PCASS technology was changed from "Portable" to "Preliminary" Credibility Assessment Screening System.

In addition, I asked if Lafayette Instrument had ever produced a version of PCASS for DoD that did not feature a yellow light to indicate an "inconclusive" reading and, if the company had, I asked for an explanation of the change.

Regarding wireless headsets, I asked if they are considered "standard equipment" for use during PCASS examinations and for an explanation of the changes in thinking/practice that have taken place regarding the use of wireless headsets during PCASS examinations. In addition, I asked if any PCASS studies involving the wearing of wireless headsets had been conducted.

I asked how many PCASS devices Lafayette Instrument has sold to DoD and if the company is able to sell PCASS devices to anyone other than DoD, adding, "If not, why not?"

Related to that, I asked, "Under what authority does DoD have the ability to restrict a private company from selling its goods or services for a system such as PCASS?"

Finally, I asked them to "identify and provide the specific DoD regulation or DoD directive that restricts Lafayette Instrument from selling PCASS to U.S. law enforcement agencies."

Not surprisingly, I received a sort of cold-shoulder treatment from officials at DITCO-Scott and DIA Headquarters. Gerry Brooks, a paralegal at DITCO-Scott, sent me down the FOIA route to obtain answers to the nine questions I directed to him. Meanwhile, DIA's Colonel Veale gave me two choices in response to 18 questions sent to him.

"Given the depth of detail of your project and my understanding of DoD's standard procedure for detailed book queries," the lieutenant colonel wrote, "I believe you should complete the book project support process."

From my Air Force experience, I knew the book project route would slow down substantially the progress of my effort, so I turned that down and went with the second option, FOIA.

In response to my request of July 18, 2012, I received a vague reply letter from Alesia Y. Williams, chief of DIA's FOIA staff, and fired back a reply.

"Unfortunately, you did not comply with federal law (see below) by providing a specific date of completion," I wrote, before citing the section of federal law that, in many more words, says that she had to provide me with a specific date upon which a determination was expected to be dispatched if it was expected to take more than the ten days provided by an extension of the basic 20-day FOIA requirement.

"Please respond ASAP with an actual specific date of completion instead of a vague 'when we get around to it' answer," I closed my message.

Almost 90 days would pass before I heard from Williams again.

"Your request is currently in the Awaiting Response Queue; #371 of 385," she wrote in a letter dated October 18, 2012. "Our current administrative workload is 1,112 open FOIA requests."

During a phone conversation I initiated five days later, I learned from Williams that I should expect to wait at least six months for my request to receive an initial determination. From experience, however, I knew actual answers to my questions could take longer -- or never come at all.

Worth noting, I also forwarded nine of the 18 questions to Fausett, my tight-lipped contact at Lafayette Instrument, believing them to be questions company officials should be able to answer. I received no answers.

"Now, back to your originally-scheduled program which continues, in progress."

# CHAPTER SEVENTEEN:
## More 'Warts'

At the same time The Oklahoma Study was progressing and more "warts" were beginning to show on the reputation of the polygraph, polygraph loyalists inside DoD commissioned a survey of U.S. law enforcement end users of CVSA®.

Conducted during the month of October 2006 by Dodd & Associates, the survey involved contacting people who possessed almost 1,500 combined years experience as police officers, had some 500 years of CVSA® experience and had conducted almost 15,000 CVSA® exams.

When NITV officials learned from multiple concerned law enforcement sources that the study was taking place without NITV's knowledge, they contacted Robert Dodd, the principal at the Gambrills, Maryland-based survey firm.

They said Dodd told them two things: his company had been subcontracted by a major defense contractor to conduct the survey for the federal government, and DoDPI had been assigned to oversee his work.

To his credit, they also said, Dodd insisted he would conduct the survey impartially and provide NITV with a copy of his final report regardless of who had requested the survey.

Based on assurances they said they received from Dodd, NITV officials advised concerned CVSA® end users in the law enforcement community who had been contacted by Dodd that they should cooperate.

NITV officials said several months passed during which they had not received a copy of the survey, so they contacted Dodd. In turn, they said, Dodd advised he had completed the survey and forwarded the results to the defense contractor.

Most importantly, NITV officials said, Dodd told them that he had been expressly prohibited by representatives of the defense contractor from sharing survey results with anyone at NITV.

When contacted by phone, Dodd confirmed that the account given by NITV officials seemed accurate.

NITV officials proceeded to request a copy of the report from DoD. After DoD officials ignored their request, they contacted the office of U.S. Representative Lincoln Diaz-Balart in June 2007 and requested assistance from the Florida Republican in obtaining a copy of the survey results.

Using the power of his office, Congressman Diaz-Balart was able to obtain a copy of the survey results, dated March 30, 2007, and forwarded it to NITV officials.

The results were so overwhelmingly positive about CVSA® that it quickly became apparent that loyalists at Polygraph Headquarters and the Army G2 (Intelligence) had wanted to bury them.

Approximately 86 percent of survey respondents indicated they thought CVSA® was either "very effective" or "extremely effective" in detecting stress.

Eighty-four percent believed their initial training from NITV had been either "very effective" or "extremely effective," but none characterized is as "not effective" or "slightly effective."

Seventy-five percent of CVSA® deception-indicated results were verified by obtaining confessions, survey

168

respondents reported, and CVSA® was cited as having "a remarkably low error rate" in the survey with respondents reporting a false-positive rate well below one percent.

"It is clear that the majority of the survey respondents believe the CVSA is a useful tool," Dodd concluded. "Key factors in this usefulness appear to be its ease of use, timeliness, affordability, and ability to help convince guilty subjects to confess. It appears to be very helpful in clearing cases."

Despite the pro-CVSA® results of the Dodd survey and the growing list of negatives tied to the polygraph, DoD officials remained intent on blocking all roads leading to CVSA®.

# CHAPTER EIGHTEEN:
## 'Hey guy' (Part Two)

Three months after the official "birth" of PCASS and more than a year after the first email message about The Oklahoma Study was exchanged between NIJ's Crossland and OU's Professor Damphousse, progress on the study continued.

"I've got the peer reviewers pretty much lined up," wrote Crossland in an email message to the professor July 21, 2006. "Don't feel pressured though because *[sic]* we're still ahead of the game time wise but...we really do need to put this thing to bed soon. Just give me a date so I can ensure that I'm here to process it and get it out to the reviewers."

On September 7, 2006, Moore sent an email to Professor Damphousse.

"Are we (I use that word loosely) going to be finished with the study before 10/17?" she asked, adding that, if they were not going to be finished by then, she would need to file a periodic progress report with the ODMHSAS Institutional Review Board (IRB), a body that serves as the general oversight board for the agency on research-related matters.

On October 4, 2006, Professor Damphousse replied to Moore.

"Sorry for the delay," he wrote. "We interviewed 331. We got urine samples from 325. BTW, 67.7% tested positive for something.... Right on par with the old ADAM numbers..."

In a mid-afternoon message 26 days later, Pointon asked Professor Damphousse what time he wanted to get together that evening for a discussion or if he was "completely wiped out from your all nighter last nite? You didn't call with questions *[sic]* so I hope that is a good sign."

On November 13, 2006, Crossland applied pressure on the professor.

"How's the draft final report?" she asked, apparently mindful that the project's fall deadline was going to be impossible to meet. "I really need it. You're a month and half past due at this point and we need to have it so it can be peer reviewed before the end date shows a delinquent status."

"I will fold their (L&D) stuff into mine and have it to you by next Monday," Professor Damphousse responded the same day, referring to researchers Pointon and Upchurch as "L&D." "Sorry for the delay."

Less than three hours later, the professor passed along Crossland's sense of urgency in a message to Pointon and another addressee, presumably Upchurch, whose identity I could not confirm.

"Folks: Looks like we need to get our stuff together pretty quick," he wrote. "I told her we would get a draft to her by NEXT Monday (i.e., one week from now). I will work on getting my stuff done but I really need you all to get your part done as quickly as possible.

"As I said last week," he continued, "just take what you have for your American Society of Criminology *[sic]*[67] presentation and write it up. Basically, I need a 'how it works' section and a 'methodology' section. I have written the lit review and I am working on the results/discussion section. Thanks for all your hard work."

Four days passed until Pointon asked Professor Damphousse about the format in which he would like her information submitted, closing her message with "thanks and I will holla tomorrow before we email you our draft okie dokie smokie!!!"

At 9:33 p.m. November 19, 2006, Pointon sent a 12-page message that included links to, and information from, the V-Worldwide and NITV web sites as well as five pages of slide thumbnails from the presentation referred to six days earlier by Professor Damphousse.

Two days later, Pointon asked the professor if he had sent off the final report yet.

"I think I can make this work," he replied the same day. "Looks pretty good right now."

In an early-morning message five days later, Crossland informed Professor Damphousse, Moore and Sheila Tillery, an ODMHSAS grants management specialist assisting with the project, that she had two issues in need of attention.

"First, the quarterly financial report for this grant was not submitted on November 14 as required placing this grant in delinquent status," Crossland wrote. "I had sent two previous emails regarding the matter but haven't heard back from anyone. If at all possible, can you please upload that document as soon as possible?

"Second, the draft final technical report is seriously overdue. Kelly, we need that report for immediate peer review. As it stands today, there is no way that this report will be able to be peer reviewed internally and externally and revised by you before the project's end of December 31, 2006. I'm amenable to extending the end date but only after the two items mentioned above are submitted and reviewed."

Crossland ended her message by asking the professor to let her know the status and timetable for those items.

Three hours later, Professor Damphousse apologized for the delay.

"My bad on the draft of the technical report," he wrote. "I am very close to completing (the technical report)." In addition, he let her know Moore would be handling the financial report.

Fifteen days passed, and the professor reported to Crossland.

"Still no word from L&D and Becki is out of town, so I am just going to finish up their part and send this to you," he wrote before explaining he was on his way to Lawton, Oklahoma, for the weekend and promising he would finish up the report there and send it to Crossland that Sunday.

That Sunday -- December 17, 2006 -- came and went along with 16 more days. Then, more than four months after the original loose deadline established by Crossland for completing the final report, Professor Damphousse submitted the draft technical report to Crossland January 3, 2007. It would be the first of many messages exchanged during the weeks that followed.

Four days later, Crossland replied to the professor, informing him that she had had to let the grant "go delinquent" and would work on a no-cost extension in order to get it back on track.

A short time later, Professor Damphousse apologized again and explained the delay was due, in part, to the fact that, unbeknownst to him, one of his key people had "disappeared in early December." In turn, Crossland shared "Final Progress

Report Requirements" with Professor Damphousse, and the project was back on track.

Via email January 11, 2007, Crossland reminded the professor that the Final Progress Report was due in 19 days.

On January 15, 2007, she informed him the draft technical report was being peer reviewed and should be returned to him by early February. At that point, she explained he would have 30 days from receipt to get her the final technical report.

On January 30, 2007, Professor Damphousse forwarded the final progress report to Moore and her ODMHSAS colleagues and instructed them to upload it to NIJ's GMS before the day ended. Shortly after 2 o'clock that afternoon, the uploading task was completed.

During the days that followed, Crossland asked the professor via email if he would have some time to discuss peer reviews of the study during a conference call February 15, 2007. She also opened the door to other opportunities.

Crossland asked Professor Damphousse if he would like to write an article about The Oklahoma Study for the *NIJ Journal* and outlined how he could provide a skeleton upon which an editor/writer would build a complete article of 800 to 2,000 words.

"I was just thinking about publication possibilities this morning (I spent last night working on my annual evaluation)," the ambitious professor replied. "I am considering seeking a promotion to full professor and need to get some stuff out."

He closed his message by thanking Crossland for her help on the project.

"You know we could not have done it without you," he wrote.

Truer words were never spoken.

On February 12 and 19, 2007, Crossland forwarded three peer reviews of the draft final report for Professor Damphousse "to ponder."

\* \* \*

Before delving into details of those peer reviews, it's important to understand the process that was in place not only on July 28, 2010, but also at the time The Oklahoma Study was reviewed.

I learned by perusing the NIJ website that, as the product of a government-funded research effort, the findings of The Oklahoma Study had had to survive the peer review process before they could be published. In addition, I learned the process via which federal government agencies doled out grant money was, at that time, both open and secretive.

It was "open" in the sense that anyone could register as a peer reviewer to assess grant applications, according to details that appeared on the NIJ website more than three years after The Oklahoma Study was published and have since been replaced with new details[68].

NIJ was seeking "reviewers from diverse backgrounds and regions who have relevant expertise and experience" in at least one of more than a dozen crime- or criminology-related fields, ranging from "crime control and prevention research" to "violence and victimization research."

Before beginning their work, those selected had to participate in an orientation telephone call during which their roles and responsibilities were outlined and the background and purpose of the grant program were made clear.

They were told some NIJ reviews were conducted remotely while others involved in-person meetings and they would score ten to 15 applications within a two- to four-week period and be paid $125 for each application reviewed.

When I tried to find out from NIJ officials the identities and qualifications of the peers who reviewed The Oklahoma Study, they offered nothing; hence, the use of the word, secretive, above.

Using FOIA and Open Records Act requests, however, I was able to find out what peer reviewers had observed about the study.

Most noteworthy, according to the first reviewer who had deemed the study "very relevant," was that the study lacked a "real-world" setting and jeopardy.

"The use of a 'real-world' setting for the study is purported to allow for a sense of jeopardy to occur in the participants, simulating the 'deception detection' response," he wrote. "Such a response is then supposedly detected by the VSA systems employed in the study. However, if the participant is not worried about getting caught (in his or her deception) or is pretending to lie, as there are no real consequences, the VSA software will not be able to detect deception.

"Thus, a potential confound for this study is that, despite the researchers best efforts, there is still no true consequence for lying as participants were informed that 'the interview could not be used to harm them in any way during their stay in the facility or at a later date.'

"Would not this knowledge on the part of the participant possibly remove the sense of jeopardy or 'lower the stakes' for lying, thus reducing the chances for the VSA systems to be able to detect potential deception?" he asked. "In other words, although arrestees may indeed be deceptive about recent drug use during the interview, is it likely that some of the effect is lost due to removal of a penalty for lying during the study interview?"

The second reviewer, who rated the study's overall quality as "between poor and good" and its relevance "between minimal and moderate," argued that questions about key features of the study design as implemented and about the analysis make it difficult to determine precisely the connection between results and findings.

Specifically, he pointed out that participants in the study "were <u>not</u> stressed by the questions, and the lying that they did was not because they were stressed but rather just because they lie a lot."

In essence, the first two reviewers agreed that The Oklahoma Study's lack of jeopardy -- an essential element NITV officials and CVSA® end users insist must be present for their technology to be effective -- had rendered it fatally flawed.

The third reviewer, who also characterized the study as "very relevant," noted that the low-cost qualitative urine drug tests used during the study can be somewhat prone to false-positive results.

Unfortunately, Professor Damphousse responded to only one criticism -- something to do with the first reviewer's concerns about inter-rater reliability -- and ignored the "elephants in the room" that were lack of jeopardy and low-quality urine tests.

* * *

On February 14, 2007, one day after he received Reviews #1 and #3 and five days before receiving Review #2, Professor Damphousse sent an email message to Pointon.

In addition to asking her if she had had a chance to read the draft final report he had already submitted to Crossland, he asked his research assistant if she "could drop off the two laptops (and the other equipment) and the KayTen credit card."

Following a "Thanks!" he added, "My laptop crashed two weeks ago and I need to use one of the VSA ones next week."

On March 14, 2007, Crossland sent another email message to Professor Damphousse.

"Hey guy...how are things?" she wrote. "I just wanted to check in and see how the final report is going. When do you think I'll be able to get it?"

"Tina: I am flying to Seattle today - be back Saturday," he replied a couple of hours later. "Long story... Brent said 'we really need to go present at Academy of Criminal Justice Sciences *[sic]* - we'll bring our kids.' he is on the program committee and he felt compelled. I normally never go there but signed up. Two weeks ago, he told me he could not make it. Now I am going on my own. Oh well." *NOTE: I believe, but could not confirm, that "Brent" mentioned in this email exchange is Brent L. Smith, an academic colleague with whom Professor Damphousse has worked on several projects, dating back as far as 1999 when Smith was at the University of Alabama-Birmingham and Damphousse was getting his feet wet at the University of Oklahoma.*

"You *[sic]* know me..." Professor Damphousse continued. "The paper is never finished. I have done all that I care to do. I have asked Bec and D and L to read it and give me comments. L finally brought over all the stuff (computers etc) on Monday *[sic]* (she was needing a reference from me) but none of the promised comments on the paper. No time to read it... Bec wrote yesterday that she had skimmed the paper but had not had time to read it... Oh well.

"Will Wednesday *[sic]* work for getting it in to you? I should probably just say Monday. Kel"

"Poor guy...always left holding the bag," Crossland wrote in reply an hour later. "I think you need a break. How about you take all the time you need so long as I have the report by March 30th?"

Ten days ahead of the latest final report deadline, Crossland shared information with Professor Damphousse about NIJ's Annual Summer Conference that was set to take place in July 2007.

Notably, Crossland explained to the professor how she and her colleagues had replied to a request five months earlier to submit proposals for panel discussions to be held at the conference.

"We submitted a proposed panel entitled, 'Liar, Liar, Liar: An Examination of Deception Technology Used in Criminal Justice Environments' (title to be finalized by panel)," Crossland wrote.

After noting that she had attached a copy of the panel abstract for him to review, Crossland added that the panel had since been approved by the NIJ director and invited Professor Damphousse to participate.

I suppose it doesn't matter much that the final final report for The Oklahoma Study had not yet been written and was, in fact, still months away at the time Crossland submitted the panel idea, "Liar, Liar, Liar," with Professor Damphousse as a participant.

Still, the timing of that submission made me wonder if the professor would have lost his seat on the panel *if* The

Oklahoma Study's final report had produced different findings, such as showing CVSA® on par with or superior to polygraph.

\* \* \*

On April 2, 2007, two days after the date that would later appear on the cover page of The Oklahoma Study and more than seven months after the original hoped-for completion date of the study's final report, Professor Damphousse sent an email to "Laur, Deid, and Beck" about the long-overdue final report needed by Crossland.

"I still have not heard from any of you regarding any comments on the Final Report," the professor wrote. "I am sending it at noon today, rain or shine. If you have ANYthing, please send it to me asap and I will try to incorporate it. Thanks. Have a great week! :-) Kelly"

Twenty-five more days passed, and Crossland emailed Professor Damphousse about the final report and about the publishing possibilities she had raised two months earlier.

"I know you said you were sending it but I'm hoping to get this thing processed quickly," she wrote. "Also, the folks within NIJ want to get an article published on the implications quickly. The idea you had [sic] mentioned has the most promise, that is, the enormous amount of resources spent by (law enforcement) on these items without any result. Are you still interested in drafting a first draft or should I have the writers do that and you just edit it? Let me know."

"Tina: you probably learned that I am outta the office until Monday... I am actually in Canada," replied the professor, a native of Canada who told me he obtained U.S. citizenship shortly after the attacks of September 11, 2001. "Long story. Sorry for the delay, I was waiting for OU (Institutional Review

Board) approval before formalizing the switch on the cover page. I don't guess it matters in the end. I get back in town Monday *[sic]* and if all goes well I will get the stuff to you then. Tuesday at the latest."

Exactly what switch was made to the cover page and what role the OU IRB played in formalizing it and other parts of the study remains unclear.

On May 1, 2007, at 8:12 a.m., Crossland sent a "high-importance" email message to Professor Damphousse and Moore "about closing out your NIJ Grant #2005-IJ-CX-0047."

Most importantly, she noted, "the final quarterly report is due by close of business on May 15, 2007 that should indicate a zero balance as any remaining funds will be deobligated. As of today, our system shows a total of $51,468.86 left in your account. When submitted this document, please make sure to indicate that this it is the FINAL report."

The following morning, Professor Damphousse queried Moore via email.

"Beck: Do you still owe me $50,000?" he wrote. "I could use it!"

"Oh. Here I was hoping that I could have it," Moore replied. "We originally budgeted for 2 consultants on the VSA and your original budget was higher because you were going to contract for the UAs" -- that is, urinalysis tests.

On May 21, 2007, more than seven weeks *after* the date appearing on the cover page of the final published report and more than eight months after its original hoped-for completion date, Professor Damphousse emailed Crossland again.

"Here, at long last, is the final report," he wrote. "I kept putting off re-doing the executive summary. I finally just up and did it. I hope these corrections work for you and your reviewers. Thanks again for your patience. Like all papers, I suppose, this thing just never seems 'done enough.' I am grateful that it is better today than it was before the first review."

Crossland acknowledged receipt in a same-day reply that included a directive to Professor Damphousse: "Now breathe :)"

Later that day, the professor sent another email to Crossland. Attached to it was a smaller PDF version of the report and a message.

"Whew whew whew whew whew whew whew whew whew," he wrote. "(sorry for being so late with this. It is all my fault but I was pretty torqued that I got NO help from B, L, or D," he wrote, referring to Moore, Pointon and Upchurch by the first letters of their first names. "I sent it to B and - after two months - she said 'looks good.' *[sic]* I didn't even get that from L&D. So, whenever I went to work on it, I got this mental block and put it off. "Maybe *[sic]* I will hear something from them today. At the same time, I kept thinking 'jerk, you're doing the same thing to Tina.' Sorry about that.)."

He ended his message with an unusual signature block -- "KelBel."

Early the next day, Crossland fired off another message to Professor Damphousse.

"I understand. I knew there was drama," she wrote. "And we all have had similar things happen so I completely empathize. The good thing is it is over with and you don't have to worry about it. That being said, you should be proud. Everyone seems to be really happy with the report/project.

Most important, OS&T (our toughest critics) seem very pleased."

Crossland went on to explain she was having people in the NIJ publications department draft an article about The Oklahoma Study for submission to *Police Chief*, a magazine published by the *International Association of Chiefs of Police* (IACP), and in *NIJ Journal* at a later date.

"Don't worry," she added, "the drafts will be reviewed by you and me for accuracy and the authorship will go to you, no one else!"

Another 18 days passed before Crossland emailed the professor again. In the subject line of her message was the loaded question, "Can you say NIJ Journal Article????"

"As I mentioned earlier," she wrote, "the NIJ Journal approved my idea for a NIJ Journal Article in regards to the VSA study findings with a focus on the investment LE has made with little proof that the technology works.

"Because we thought the journal queue was backed up, we decided we should write an article for Police Chief and reprint it in the NIJ Journal at a later date. Well...the Communications Division and David Hagy (NIJ's Director) want it in the Journal sooner.

"They want it in the December 2007 Issue. So here's my question...do you want to write the article (1500 to 1700 words) yourself? If so, we have to have it by August 10th? If not, we're going to have to ship it out. I know you are very busy so just let me know."

Without question, Crossland's messages to the professor indicated her colleagues at NIJ were pleased with the findings of The Oklahoma Study. Unfortunately for NIJ leaders, the article[69] would not appear in *NIJ Journal* until March 2008.

Like many of the previous study deadlines, the one associated with publishing the article was busted.

Regardless, The Oklahoma Study was finished, NIJ officials were pleased, and polygraph loyalists everywhere were anxious to get their hands on this new "ammunition" they could use toward, in Colonel Bell's words, "eliminating the challenger."

\* \* \*

The copy of The Oklahoma Study I obtained in April 2009 appeared quite thorough at first glance and gave the impression that at least half of the people involved in the research effort worked on behalf of the university or, at a minimum, had the tacit endorsement of administrators at the Sooner State school most famous for its football team's seven national championships. Remember, though, the cover -- and changes to it -- had been approved by the university's IRB, according to Professor Damphousse.

Listed on The Oklahoma Study's cover page were four names and affiliations: Kelly R. Damphousse, University of Oklahoma; Laura Pointon, University of Oklahoma; Deidra Upchurch, KayTen Research and Development; and Rebecca K. Moore, Oklahoma Department of Mental Health and Substance Abuse Services.

I would learn via several email exchanges with OU Vice President of Public Affairs Catherine F. Bishop between February 2012 and September 2012 that university officials were more at ease with distancing themselves from the project than endorsing it.

"Because of their expertise, it is quite normal for faculty members to consult with companies outside of the University of Oklahoma," she wrote on one such occasion. "It is also not unusual for a faculty member to own a private business or company."

In response to other study-related questions, however, she wrote, "These are not questions for me to answer. The research was conducted by a private firm."

The fine print at the bottom of the report's cover page showed it was made possible through a $232,200 grant (#2005-IJ-CX-0047) from NIJ to ODMHSAS.

After learning that funding for the study had come from a pool of discretionary funds awarded by NIJ through a noncompetitive process, I found myself curious to learn what had qualified the study for a noncompetitive award.

When I visited the "Guidelines Regarding Non-Competitive Awards" section[70] of the NIJ website July 28, 2010, I learned the research proposal should have had to clear at least one of the following hurdles in order to be approved for NIJ funding: (1) NIJ would have had to determine ODMHSAS was the only responsible applicant who could perform the work of the proposed award; (2) The NIJ Director would have had to determine in writing that exigent, urgent, or other compelling circumstances existed to make it in the public interest to make the award non-competitively; (3) ODMHSAS would have had to be specified by an appropriations act or other applicable federal law; and/or (4) A House, Senate or Conference Report accompanying an appropriations act or other law would have had to recommend the award to a particular recipient, and the award would have had to be made consistent with applicable law, including any applicable executive orders.

Less than one percent of the NIJ's annual awards through fiscal year 2009 had been dished out under the "noncompetitive" label, according to information found on the same site.

Uncertain as to which hurdle(s) The Oklahoma Study award had crossed on its way to qualifying for this type of funding, I reached out to NIJ Communications Chief Jolene Hernon and requested a copy of the NIJ Director's determination in writing that the project had been deemed worthy of noncompetitive status. That, too, took place July 28, 2010.

Fifty days later, I received a response -- but not from Hernon. Instead, it came from Thomas E. Feucht, Ph.D. and NIJ's executive senior science advisor.

Via email, Dr. Feucht asked if we could talk by phone. I responded, telling him I would prefer to have his comments in writing.

Four more days passed before I received his explanation, in writing, that no documentation of the NIJ director's "determination in writing" was available, because the grant had been made in 2005 -- before NIJ policies required written documentation on noncompetitive grants.

Apparently, Dr. Feucht expected me to believe that, prior to 2005, NIJ wasn't required to keep records of approval for studies costing hundreds of thousands of dollars. Finding that difficult to swallow, I posed another question to the NIJ executive.

I asked Dr. Feucht if the guidelines used in granting noncompetitive awards had changed since January 1, 2005. In reply, he offered the kind of carefully-worded written response that would make any bureaucrat proud.

"NIJ is committed to a competitive process for awarding grants," he wrote. "While more than 90 percent of NIJ's research grants are made in response to open solicitations, in accordance with its statutory authority, the NIJ director has always reserved the authority to award grants non-competitively.

"New agency guidelines instituted last year," he continued, referring to 2009, "require program managers to provide written justification for each non-competitive award. However, the authority for making non-competitive awards has not changed."

Dr. Feucht offered nothing to suggest the award recipient was special or uniquely qualified to carry out the study; nothing in the form of a determination in writing by the NIJ director; and no evidence that some Legislative or Executive Branch action had authorized funding for the study. In short, the NIJ official's responses left me more curious than ever.

Worth noting: Almost a year after the exchange with Dr. Feucht, during which I also asked questions about the peer-review process and pointed out flaws in the publicly-available information about it on the agency's website, NIJ totally revamped the process and unveiled it as a new "pilot project" during the 2011 NIJ Conference[71] in Arlington, Virginia, June 20-22, 2011.

* * *

Beyond The Oklahoma Study's cover page, a one-page abstract offered conclusions the authors could have boiled down to six words, "Both VSA programs show poor validity."

One person disheartened by those conclusions is Bill Endler.

Retired since 2000 after more than 30 years in law enforcement that included stints as chief of police in several

Indiana communities, Endler said he stumbled upon CVSA®
by accident soon after arriving in Syracuse, Indiana, to serve as
the city's police chief.

Though prepared to purchase a polygraph, he learned the
department already owned CVSA® equipment (i.e., a laptop
computer and software) and decided he would give it a try. His
first step involved attending a CVSA® training class in Fort
Wayne, Indiana, in June 1996.

"I just fell in love with (CVSA), because it was so much
easier to use," he said, careful to note that he doesn't bad-
mouth the polygraph.

"I was successful with polygraph," he said before
explaining he had used polygraph from 1983 until 2000 and
had used both technologies during the last four years of his law
enforcement career, 1996 to 2000.

"I had a prosecuting attorney who wasn't keen on the
CVSA," Endler explained, "so I would do a polygraph in the
morning and a CVSA in the afternoon.

"What I say, basically, is, 'If you are a good interrogator
now, this will make you better,'" Endler continued. "That's
really what it's about."

Endler's experience pays off when he's teaching classes
to new and veteran CVSA® examiners, he said, because he's
able to share stories of how the technology has worked for him.

In addition to being one of the world's leading experts on
CVSA®, Endler holds two other distinctions: He is the NITV
staffer who taught Oklahoma researchers Pointon and
Upchurch how to conduct CVSA® exams when they traveled
to Florida for training, and he is the expert to whom the duo
sent copies of their CVSA® output files (a.k.a., "charts")
during the data-collection phase of The Oklahoma Study for a
no-cost review.

Endler's calm tone of voice during a 2012 interview made it apparent to me that his real-world law enforcement experience -- coupled, perhaps, with the passage of time -- had taught him to control his emotions when discussing weighty subjects. The same holds true for his written words.

Endler penned a "To Whom It May Concern" letter in which he expressed his concerns about how Pointon and Upchurch had done their jobs.

"I worked with them during class and after class to give them extra instructions to carry out the study that they intended to do," Endler explained in the letter dated November 3, 2009. "As per my discussions with them during training, I telephoned them on numerous occasions prior to the study offering them assistance of any kind.

"Occasionally," he continued, "I would receive a call back from them; however, they were not interested in my help. As a number of months passed since they attended the basic CVSA examiner course prior to conducting their study, I offered several times to fly to Oklahoma at the NITV's expense to assist them with conducting their first CVSA examinations. Again they were not interested in NITV's assistance."

In addition to refusing assistance, he pointed out that Pointon and Upchurch forwarded charts to Endler that were produced during the CVSA® exams. Due to technical errors in the way the inexperienced examiners conducted the tests, those charts were not usable and had the effect of rendering half of the examinations they conducted invalid.

Endler also cited as "substantial" the amount of time that elapsed between the time the women attended the basic CVSA® examiners course and when testing was done.

It "calls into question their ability to properly conduct CVSA examinations," he wrote.

Though Endler did not mention it in his letter, the text of an email message he received February 6, 2006, reveals Professor Damphousse seemed comfortable with -- or, perhaps, naïve about -- his researchers' post-training abilities.

Obtained via FOIA, the professor's message was sent in reply to Endler, who had offered to travel to Oklahoma to assist Pointon and Upchurch with the testing.

"I would hate for you to have to fly out here (although I really appreciate the offer)," Professor Damphousse wrote before adding a note about his researchers. "They have been keeping in practice and seem very comfortable with the equipment, so I guess they were trained well...."

When it came to identifying the most-serious flaw in the study, Endler pointed to the lack of jeopardy that had been pointed out by reviewers of the study proposal and, later, the study findings.

"The researchers attempted to create jeopardy in the individuals they tested (known/suspected drug abusers) by offering them a candy bar if they beat the test," Endler wrote. "Any CVSA examiner trained by the NITV knows that jeopardy is only created in real life situations, when there is a fear in the individual of punishment or consequence."

Remember, according to the final report, study participants were told the interviews could not be used to harm them and that those "who completed the interview and provided a urine sample were given a candy bar as an incentive."

In other words, Endler pointed out, the jeopardy required for an effective exam simply was not present.

* * *

Unaware at the time that Endler had written his letter 99 days earlier and not yet realizing my interest in this story would lead to writing this book, I began corresponding with Professor Damphousse the afternoon of February 10, 2010.

I explained in an initial email message to the professor that I was a freelance journalist "investigating the federal government's use, primarily by the military, of portable, hand-held polygraph devices in combat zones. Related to that, I'm seeking out experts who have conducted research on either polygraph or any of the competing technologies to help me better understand what's on the market."

Included in the message were eight questions that were followed by another message containing one additional question six days later.

Eight days after sending my first message to Professor Damphousse, he replied with answers to many, but not all, of my questions.

When asked how he would respond to individuals who say the study was flawed by its lack of jeopardy, by the failure of researchers to follow mandatory protocols for conducting CVSA® examinations, and by researchers' use of less-reliable urine-testing equipment, he responded by saying he had "not seen these critiques in the scientific literature."

Beyond that, he offered a brief response about his choice of a urine-testing tool.

"As I understand it," he wrote, "GC-MS is especially useful when determining drug concentrations in urine (which was not one of the study's objectives) while EMIT has very good sensitivity (is able to detect presence of a drug in urine – an objective of the study). I am attaching an article that favorably compares EMIT to GC-MS and Online KIMS (another drug-screening assay)."

Published in 2006, the article[72] he attached was described by its authors as exploring "the efficacy of two commercially available drug-screening assays" used during testing for the ADAM program, something with which Professor Damphousse had had much experience.

I wouldn't find out until long after my ice-breaking email exchange with the professor that his response to my question about his choice of a urinalysis-testing method was quite different than the explanation he had given Pointon more than four years earlier.

In an email message to Pointon, dated December 12, 2005, Professor Damphousse used the words, "long story having mostly to do with cost."

Before our virtual conversation ended, Professor Damphousse provided a phone number at which I could contact him to learn more about his involvement in The Oklahoma Study.

At approximately 1:30 p.m. February 19, 2010, I reached him at his Norman office.

The call began cordially, and the interview commenced softly with me asking Professor Damphousse to explain how the process of getting grant money works.

The professor, who had been named "President's Associates Presidential Professor" and promoted to associate dean for OU's College of Arts & Sciences a short time after completing The Oklahoma Study, drew upon his time spent as a faculty member -- during which he said he "used to write a lot of grants" -- to explain "generally how it works."

"Typically, funding agencies put out requests for proposals," he explained, "and that comes in various forms, and researchers -- often times people who are at universities, but sometimes people who are at organizations like the Rand Corporation and so on -- will apply for funding.

"There's a review process, then a decision made by the funding agency as to where they will send their money."

Asked to describe his involvement in obtaining the NIJ grant for The Oklahoma Study, he told me he had helped write the application but made no mention of the dozens of emails he had exchanged with Crossland.

When asked if he was actually involved in collecting the data for the study, he said, "Oh no, I collected the data."

After I asked if he was the person chiefly responsible for that or if someone else had been involved, he backtracked slightly.

"I supervised the data collection, although I didn't collect the data personally," Professor Damphousse said, explaining that one of the researchers was a student at the university, but not one of his students, and both had worked for him in the past.

"They went and got trained," he said, referring to Pointon and Upchurch, "and then they collected the data."

Next, I asked the professor to clarify some dollar amounts related to the NIJ grant for The Oklahoma Study. Instead of answering any questions on that topic, he directed me to Dr. Davis who, as director of Decision Support Services at ODMHSAS, had signed the original "Investigator Initiated Research Proposal."

I didn't press the issue and, instead, moved on to a discussion of KayTen's involvement in The Oklahoma Study.

Bob McCarty

"You mentioned KayTen Research was an outside firm,"
I began, fully aware at the time that Professor Damphousse was
listed as the "registered agent" of the limited-liability company
(LLC) on the Oklahoma Secretary of State's (OSoS) website[73].
"Was it typical in doing grants and research projects for you to
use an outside firm like that?"

"Typical for DMH to do that? I don't know," he
answered, referring to ODMHSAS by a condensed version of
the acronym for the state mental health agency's long name.

When I asked if KayTen had been contracted by
ODMHSAS, Professor Damphousse at first gave the
impression he couldn't remember, then something -- but not
the dozens of emails exchanged with Crossland over a 24-
month period -- seemed to dawn on him.

"I think there was... yeah, I guess that's how it would
have happened," Professor Damphousse said.

It was after I asked another question -- "Was that the only
time you ever worked with KayTen?" -- that the professor
explained his intimate ties to the firm.

"Actually, that's my company," he said, adding, "I can't
remember how it came to be, exactly who called who first. I
don't want to say the wrong thing. I just don't remember how
that worked."

Did he not want to mention Crossland's role in launching
the project and the nearly six months of dialogue and meetings
that had preceded the official announcement about NIJ
approving funding for the study or did he not remember? It
seemed as if that was the case.

My questions about KayTen continued, and Professor
Damphousse explained that he had used his company on "quite
a few" projects but couldn't remember exactly how many.

195

I asked if he was still using the company for projects.

"The company still exists," he replied. "It's an LLC. It's just a... basically a consulting company, but it's basically me."

Before popping any of the interview questions to the professor, I had already learned by reviewing publicly-available records on the aforementioned OSoS website that KayTen's LLC status had been "canceled" July 1, 2007. In addition, I had sought confirmation of that fact by contacting an agency official by phone. The gentleman with whom I spoke told me the word, "canceled," indicated the responsible person for the LLC had either failed to pay the annual $25 registration/renewal fee or had filed papers of dissolution.

Despite knowing what I know about KayTen's status prior to the interview, the professor's statements don't make him guilty of any crime; rather, they simply raise questions in my mind: "Why had he been so slow to let me know about his involvement as a principle at KayTen?" and "Is it possible the professor did not know his company no longer existed, according to the state of Oklahoma?"

Rather than press the issue, I moved on to other topics so as to not chance derailing the interview prematurely.

"Earlier, you said OU didn't receive any funds from the grant," I said, introducing my next topic area. "Does that mean you didn't receive any compensation (from OU) other than your faculty salary? How does that work?"

"This work was done outside of OU work, so it wasn't done as part of my job as an OU employee," he said.

"Fair enough," I thought.

A discussion followed about items listed on his *curriculum vitae* (CV), the academic equivalent of a resume that was available on his OU faculty web page at the time of the interview.

Professor Damphousse, according to that CV, had been a key player in 22 NIJ grant-funded studies costing taxpayers $4,453,500 -- or more than $202,000 per grant. That total included funding for The Oklahoma Study -- valued at $232,200 instead of $177,921 as shown on the aforementioned CV.

After reminding Professor Damphousse of what he had told me via email (i.e., that he had not seen critiques in the scientific literature about flaws in The Oklahoma Study), I asked him if he had seen any critiques in the scientific literature that mentioned methodology or findings of his study?

In response, he suggested I review a paper[74] published in the *International Journal of Speech, Language and the Law*.

Because I had not yet read or researched the paper, I chose not to discuss it during the interview. Later, however, I discovered two important findings about the paper published in December 2007: (1) It had been pulled from publication soon after the information it contained was challenged; and (2) It became the subject of a retraction notice and apology written by a senior editor of the *Journal*[75] one year later.

A brief discussion about the peer-review process and Professor Damphousse's understanding of how it works was followed by questions about study costs.

I pointed out to Professor Damphousse that he had mentioned costs as an important consideration when looking at the two non-polygraph technologies, but made no mention of polygraph costs in the study's final report.

"A glaring omission, perhaps?" I wondered out loud.

"Well, there are people who have studied, who have compared CVSA to the polygraph, but I wasn't really... I wasn't doing a comparison," he responded. "I was just simply evaluating those two programs. So I wasn't really comparing one to the other."

Puzzled, I replied, saying, "you described costs as 'an important consideration in appreciating the effectiveness of VSA products.'"

Around noting that he had not read his paper in a long time, he said, "Actually, I think somewhere along the line I mentioned the benefits of doing voice stress analysis was that you could do more of them in a day than you could a polygraph, because with a polygraph you could do two in a day and, obviously, you can do several very quickly with voice stress analysis. That's one of the benefits of using it. There's an implication there of cost and time and money."

* * *

A close look at cost factors associated with polygraph and CVSA® reveals several sources showing CVSA® substantially more affordable than either the traditional polygraph or the newer, portable PCASS.

One source, an easy-to-locate online report[76] published by researchers for the Virginia Board of Professional Regulations, cites a 2002 study[77] that listed the total cost of polygraph equipment and training (i.e., tuition, room and board, and salary for one student during training) at $26,073.84. The same study, however, listed equipment and training costs for CVSA® at only $11,654 -- almost $15,000 less!

198

Another source, a U.S. Air Force talking paper[78] published in 2006, reflected an estimated cost to train one polygraph examiner at $25,000, but failed to mention whether that included equipment costs.

Finally, on January 24, 2013, the APA website[79] showed polygraph costs (instrument and tuition) at $11,000 and CVSA® costs (software and tuition) at $11,290, but mentioned nothing about the training time required for polygraph (i.e., at least eight weeks at a cost of several thousand dollars to cover a trainee's room and board and salary). Neither did it mention the time required for CVSA®.

When I spoke to NITV officials in January 2013, they told me $7,895 covered the costs of CVSA® -- including a laptop computer, software and tuition -- as well as training for *two* people that now lasts only *five* days.

Even when one compares CVSA® costs to PCASS costs, the non-polygraph tool turns out to be much less expensive than the polygraph offshoot after one factors in training-related costs (i.e., trainee's room and board and salary) over time.

\* \* \*

The interview continued, but I didn't push the cost issue further. Instead, I moved on to other issues, beginning with the urinalysis tests about which we had already exchanged email messages.

When I asked Professor Damphousse why he did not use the GC/MS urinalysis test he had described in the final report as the "gold standard," he blamed his choice on wanting to be "as efficient as possible" and on input received from people he said knew more about urinalysis than he did. He did not, however, mention the difficulties his researchers had had finding a lab to do the testing or anything else about the events he had summarized in his December 12, 2005, message (i.e., "long story having mostly to do with cost") to Pointon.

After a brief detour, I raised another serious subject.

"If you became convinced that something in one of your studies -- this one or another -- was flawed," I asked, "what would you do to correct it? Or would you?"

"That's a good question," he replied. "Typically, how that's done is that somebody writes an article refuting the findings."

After using a few dozen words to elaborate on the topic, he boiled his answer down to a dozen plus two: "If there are errors, that's how that gets pointed out in the scientific world."

Pressing the issue, I pointed the professor to page 31 of The Oklahoma Study's final report and the subject of jeopardy -- or lack thereof -- that had been raised by two of the reviewers of the study's pre-funding proposal.

"You say, 'The subjects were informed that the interview could not be used to harm them in any way during their stay in the facility or at a later date.' Do you understand that jeopardy had to be part of the equation?" I asked.

"I'm pretty sure I described that issue in the report," Professor Damphousse replied before explaining that he had suggested lack of jeopardy was apparent in some earlier studies and that he thought The Oklahoma Study got "much more closer to a real-life situation" involving jeopardy.

"You're right that it's not a perfect example of jeopardy," Professor Damphousse added, "but we thought that there was some jeopardy there. We thought it was an advance over what the previous studies had done."

Bob McCarty

"What part, exactly, did you think was the jeopardy part that you included?" I countered.

"Well, the fact that people were sitting in a jail setting or being asked that, to report about previous drug activities," he replied. "We thought that there was some social jeopardy involved in that people may not want to tell other people that they used drugs recently."

The professor ended his thoughts on the topic by saying the jeopardy involved in his study was "not as straightforward as the example you provided earlier," referring to an example I had given of real-life jeopardy (i.e., a suspect in a homicide case faces the prospect of spending the rest of his life in prison or being sentenced to death). He added that such real-life jeopardy is "very difficult to replicate in a clinical setting."

Upon hearing the professor's answer, I immediately brought to his attention something Colonel Bell had said decades earlier (i.e., "Frequently, studies performed by members of the academic community are based on an attempt to create an artificial model of the real world rather than the real world itself") before asking him if he would acknowledge that creating a real-world environment is difficult.

"Absolutely!" he replied, prompting me to move on to the issue of whether mandatory protocols for conducting the exam were followed by Professor Damphousse's researchers, Pointon and Upchurch.

"I'm told that the two young ladies working on your behalf went down to get (CVSA®) training and were told they needed to implement that training soon after in order to be able to use it and also to consult with the trainers as they, you know, implement what they learned in the training," I explained, "but they did not contact anyone at the training agency for upwards of four months and had no substantial contact with them. Is that accurate or...?"

"I don't know," Professor Damphousse answered, cutting me off. "I don't know if they were told that, and I don't know how long it was before they contacted them. The timing may be about right. I think they were trained at the end of the year, and then the data collection started early the next year, so it probably was a couple of months between training and actual implementation.

"I do recall that, to keep themselves knowledgeable about the techniques, they practiced on it periodically between training and implementation," he continued. "There probably was some lag time between training and implementation, but this is the first I've heard about that issue."

"Another (flaw) was the actual tests themselves," I said to the professor before explaining that NITV officials claimed Pointon and Upchurch had held the microphone in front of the individuals being questioned -- a "cardinal sin" of conducting a CVSA® exam -- instead of using a clip-on type of microphone less prone to movement and static discharge which effects voice patterns produced during an exam. "Were you aware of that?"

"No," Professor Damphousse said. "I haven't heard that critique either."

\* \* \*

While the professor may not have *heard* that critique, I think it's safe to say he was aware microphone-related issues had been a problem during the data-collection phase of the study. In fact, he mentioned the subject on page 90 of the final report.

"We experienced two methodological problems while conducting the research," Professor Damphousse wrote. "First, the CVSA expert reported that several of the charts that the research team had created showed signs of over-modulation resulting in their not being useable. The research team knew this was going to be a problem because they had a lot of trouble getting the microphone to work correctly.

"Unless the microphone was held directly in front of the respondent's mouth," he continued, "the CVSA instrument would not record a chart. If the microphone was held too closely to the mouth, however, the captured chart was over-modulated. That said, the research team made as many calls about deception as possible, resulting in nearly twice as much data for the novices as from the CVSA expert."

Well before the final report was published, a series of email messages exchanged the afternoon of April 12, 2006, shed even more light on the subject of microphone-related issues.

In the first message, NITV's Endler asked Professor Damphousse if Pointon and Upchurch were recording the CVSA® tests and if he could get a copy of the tape in order to try to produce better charts for them to analyze.

Professor Damphousse replied to Endler almost 90 minutes later, copying Pointon and Upchurch.

"Thanks for sending me this information," he wrote. "No, we didn't record the interviews. I spoke with Laura and she said that she and Deidre did everything they were trained to do to limit the modulation problem. I don't know what to suggest. I could have them go back and collect more data but I'm afraid we will have the same problem. If anything, the modulation problem seems to have gotten worse over time and not better as I had hoped. Is this a common problem?"

Professor Damphousse's statement about not recording the interviews is a curious one when one remembers what appeared in the narrative on page 29 of The Oklahoma Study. There, the researchers described in more detail how they had told each inmate prior to his exam that, among other things, his responses would be recorded to test how well the technologies determined stress.

The professor went on to note that his team had "good data on about 80 cases, so we will just have to go with what we have" before closing his message by thanking Endler for his interpretation of the cases.

At 3:01 p.m., Pointon replied to the professor only, appearing worried about the number of usable CVSA® charts and displaying what appeared to be a lack of understanding about how CVSA® -- and final report writing -- works.

"Are you really okay with 80 that sounds low to me I'm not so sure about that or are you thinking we just write it up in the paper," she wrote. "Can I ask one question? Did he call any of the cases inconclusive I know that he said there were all these cases with over modulation that not analyzable but the others that he called should have been either NDI (No Deception Indicated), DI (Deception Indicated), or Inconclusive (meaning not enough info either way to make a call). I just wonder about Inconclusive. You don't have to answer if you don't want to and I can explain my rationale for the question further if you like."

The professor responded to Pointon only at 4:10 p.m.

"I agree that 80 sounds low but I don't see enough improvement to warrant going back in," he wrote. "He just said 'modulation' on certain ones, DI, clipped, and NDI on others...I don't recall seeing "inconclusive."

"Don't you think that is odd that there are none out of 172 that he doesn't consider inconclusive or uncallable simply by chance?" Pointon replied 13 minutes later. "Even if they have it down to a science you would think that with that many samples there would be a certain number of inconclusives again it kinda worries me but what can we do am I being cloak and dagger now or do you see what I am saying?"

Pointon's apparent unwillingness to accept the fact that CVSA®, unlike the polygraph, does not produce "inconclusive" results runs counter to what veteran CVSA® examiners like Charlie at GITMO, Ed in Baghdad, Mike in Ohio, Endler at NITV and others know from years of experience.

The meaning behind her "cloak and dagger" comment, meanwhile, remains mysterious.

Later during the interview, I explained that a university professor from Corning, New York, had told me about a statement -- "Law enforcement will argue that it works, but they live and work in the real world and I don't" -- he claimed Professor Damphousse had made to him during a phone call the previous fall.

Professor Damphousse did not deny making that statement.

"I don't know if I said exactly that," he replied, "but I do say -- in fact, I think it's in that report -- that you have to be careful what 'works' means."

That exchange was followed by a brief discussion of the "works" issue and about something the Professor Damphousse called the "Bogus Pipeline Effect" which he said is the phenomenon that people will answer more honestly if they believe that their responses can be tested for accuracy.

Professor Damphousse concluded his remarks on the subject by explaining that his research results seemed to indicate people lied during the conduct of The Oklahoma Study less often than they did in previous studies when CVSA® was not used.

"And, so, that makes me sympathetic to people who say the program works," he explained. "I understand, I think I understand, what they mean by that."

The interview continued, and I brought up the subject of flaws in The Oklahoma Study one more time.

"You say you think you tested it as well as you could, but if your people who went through training didn't follow the steps, such as holding the microphone, which is pretty basic, doesn't that flaw the study from the beginning?"

Again, Professor Damphousse said I was the first person to raise that as a possible problem with his study. In turn, I thought back to the letter Endler had written.

"And what about tossing out the results that were a result of the mishandling, wrongly conducting the tests, such as the microphone?" I asked.

"As far as I know, we did eliminate those," Professor Damphousse said. "Those were all coded. As I recall, there were three codes: There was 'deception indicated.' Then there was "no deception indicated" and then, I can't remember the exact term that was used, but it was something like 'indecipherable,' 'unknown' or 'can't be assessed.' Those were the three options."

I didn't point it out to Professor Damphousse during the interview, but anyone familiar with CVSA® knows a properly-conducted test can produce only two possible results -- "Deceptive" or "Not Deceptive."

206

Conversely, as highlighted earlier in this book, polygraph testing produces three possible outcomes: "No Deception Indicated (NDI)," "Deception Indicated (DI)," and "No Opinion (NO)". And, again, there's Endler's letter.

When I asked Professor Damphousse if he had ever had a reason to consult with people in the polygraph community, he noted -- but did not elaborate on -- an occasion when he was required to take a polygraph exam in conjunction with employment. He did not, however, mention his friendship with a person who could qualify as a polygraph loyalist.

While perusing study-related email messages between Professor Damphousse and his primary NIJ contact months after the interview, I came across details of that friendship.

"I chatted again with my friend in psychology yesterday about her helping with the report," Professor Damphousse wrote in response to Crossland's message June 20, 2006. "Turns out, she is on her way to the national polygraph association meetings next week, so upon her return, we should be good to go. I think that she will be a big help."

Whether or not the friend provided much help remains unclear. Not unclear, however, is that he was willing to enlist the help of someone with clear ties to the polygraph community to help him write the final report for The Oklahoma Study.

The interview ended cordially, but without any substantive admission by the professor that his study might have been fatally flawed.

* * *

Three days after the interview, I began the follow-up process.

In addition to seeking clarifications and answers to new questions that had cropped up about The Oklahoma Study, I hoped to provide the professor opportunities for more input.

One topic I asked about was KayTen, the company the professor told me during the interview "still exists" despite it being listed on the OSoS website as "canceled" July 1, 2007 -- barely three months after the study was published and some 30 months before I had contacted him the first time. I simply wanted to know if the state agency's records were inaccurate or if, perhaps, he had decided to shut down the company in Oklahoma and re-establish it in another state.

On the subject of funding, I asked Professor Damphousse to provide a general breakout of how research funding for The Oklahoma Study was distributed between ODMHSAS and KayTen and how the $165,344 earmarked in the approved funding proposal ended up being used by his company? Specifically, I wanted to clear up questions I had about the disposition of $54,279 that, according to the July 14, 2005, email Crossland sent Professor Damphousse, raised the available funding amount to $232,200.

I wanted to know, because I could find no evidence that either "an expert in performing psychometric data analyses" or two "VSA experts" -- not to be confused with NITV's Endler who provided his services at no cost -- were ever procured for the study.

I also asked the professor why he opted for the less-costly urinalysis-testing option when, it appeared, he had not spent any of the grant dollars that had been made available for the aforementioned experts.

Related to the data-collection and analysis phases of the study, I asked Professor Damphousse if he might "forward via email copies of the CVSA charts" made during the tests at the Oklahoma County Detention Center.

Another concern I had centered on the date (i.e., March 31, 2007) that appeared on the cover page of The Oklahoma Study's final report.

According to copies of emails I obtained and reviewed, Professor Damphousse did not forward the final report to Crossland until May 21, 2007 -- more than seven weeks after the date that appeared on the cover page of the final published report and more than eight months after its original hoped-for completion date.

After rehashing some of the concerns highlighted earlier in this book about The Oklahoma Study, I politely challenged Professor Damphousse to describe the evidence he had to show voice stress technology does not work.

\* \* \*

While waiting for replies from the professor, I also reached out to others who had played a role in The Oklahoma Study.

First on my list to contact were Pointon and Upchurch.

After tracking down Facebook pages and phone numbers for Upchurch and Pointon, both of whom had married and taken on new names -- McCloud and Gib, respectively -- since completing their work for the professor, I reached both during a single call to Upchurch-McCloud. Unfortunately, they told me to take all of my questions to Professor Damphousse before offering an 18-word verbal addendum.

"Everything you need to know for what you're doing is in the paper," Upchurch-McCloud said. "That's what we're telling you."

Further follow-up attempts went unanswered, and I began listening once again to the same instincts that had surfaced a year earlier when CENTCOM officials had taken so long to answer my PCASS-related questions.

Even after I had let Professor Damphousse and crew know I still wanted to be fair and give them opportunities to respond to my questions, none of my post-interview inquiries garnered a single reply. As a result, I learned nothing about whether the laptop computer and related equipment had, upon completion of The Oklahoma Study, been returned to NIJ; nothing about whether or not KayTen's LLC status had, indeed, been canceled; and nothing about the manner in which $54,279 added to the original project budget had been spent -- or not.

* * *

During my unproductive wait for answers, I did find time to do a little reading, beginning with a look at the March 2008 *NIJ Journal* article[80] featuring Professor Damphousse's byline. Unfortunately, Professor Damphousse -- and/or his ghostwriter(s), I don't know who -- displayed very little of the sympathy he had told me during the interview he had for people who believe in CVSA®.

In fact, the writer of the article seemed to go out of his way to hammer home the point that CVSA® was "no better than flipping a coin when it comes to detecting deception regarding recent drug use."

As a tiny dose of sympathy, however, the writer's mention of the "bogus pipeline effect" being in play during data collection was barely evident amidst the CVSA®-directed negativity in the article.

"The hidden costs are, of course, more difficult to quantify," he wrote. "As VSA programs come under greater scrutiny--due, in part, to reports of false confessions during investigations that used VSA--the overall value of the technology continues to be questioned."

The article ended with what might be described as a "foot-stomp message" -- that is, the one its author(s) wanted readers to take home after reading it.

"Clearly," he wrote, "law enforcement administrators and policymakers should weigh all factors when deciding to purchase or use VSA technology."

Whether penned solely by Professor Damphousse or in collaboration with NIJ staffers offered up by Crossland, the article's message was one polygraph loyalists wanted, liked, and would cite as often as possible: CVSA® doesn't work, and it's not suitable as a replacement for the polygraph. *End of story!*

\* \* \*

In addition to the *NIJ Journal* article, I came across one more interesting find in the form of the course description of a class Professor Damphousse had taught at OU during the spring of 2009 -- almost two years after the study was published. The two-month course was titled, "Program Evaluation (Course Number: PSC 5143-490)."

Especially noteworthy were the first three sentences appearing in the course description I found online.

"When powerful members of society determine that a 'problem' exists, there are two options. The first is to ignore the problem and hope it goes away. The second (more

THE CLAPPER MEMO

favorable) reaction is to implement a policy or a program designed to 'fix' the problem."

The description reminds me a bit of what Colonel Bell outlined almost three decades earlier as options available to members of the polygraph community (a.k.a., "powerful members of society") as they faced the prospect of competition from CVSA® (a.k.a., "the problem").

# CHAPTER NINETEEN:
## Losing 'Teeth'

Some 40 months after The Cambone Memo had been issued and only months after The Oklahoma Study went public, then-USDI Clapper issued a memo of his own.

Why another memo? Because, according to sources close to the subject matter, The Cambone Memo had lost some of its "teeth" after its namesake resigned his position as USDI December 21, 2006, and troops in the field began using CVSA® again.

The subject line of "The Clapper Memo," dated October 29, 2007, spoke volumes: "Operational Approval of the Preliminary Credibility Assessment Screening System (PCASS)." It was in the body of the document, however, where one finds the DNI designated the polygraph and its hand-held cousin, PCASS, as the "only approved credibility assessment technologies" in DoD.

Essentially a repeat of The Cambone Memo, The Clapper Memo served to make it possible for DoD polygraph loyalists to maintain their six decades-long stranglehold on truth- and deception-detection activities within the department. At the same time, it sent a dangerous message to U.S. troops: *"Stop using CVSA!"*

One former member of the Navy SEALs, who spoke with me on the condition I not reveal his identity, said The Clapper

Memo was a contributing factor in his decision to retire from the military much earlier than he could have. Furthermore, he pulled no punches while sharing his opinion about the controversial topic.

"In my opinion, the people responsible for blocking CVSA use should face charges and do time," he wrote. "This is another issue that boils down directly to money.

"The polygraph faction knows that CVSA would make polygraph obsolete," he continued. "Too bad they can't just accept it and shift over to become certified CVSA examiners (like me). CVSA is so much easier, effective and accurate than polygraph."

Less than nine months after The Clapper Memo was issued, Admiral Eric T. Olson, SOCOM commander, entered the fray by issuing Policy Memorandum 08-11 (a.k.a., "The Olson Memo"). Dated June 16, 2008, and addressed to commanding officers of the diverse military units making up SOCOM, it repeated what had been included in the Cambone and Clapper memos and added something new in the form of a specific prohibition against using one particular type of equipment.

"In accordance with DOD and USD(I) regulations and guidance outlined in references (a) through (c) (of the memorandum)," the memo began, "the use of CVSA... is strictly prohibited under all circumstances, with no exceptions. The polygraph and the PCASS (Preliminary Credibility Assessment Screening System) are the only approved credibility assessment technologies in DOD.

"Pursuant to USD(I) policy, however, research and improvements on other potential credibility assessment tools continue to be a priority for DOD."

One retired Army Special Forces Soldier who asked that his name not appear in this book because it could negatively impact his post-military employment status, described The Olson Memo as a disservice to all who wear the uniform and shared his suspicion that the admiral had been seriously and purposefully misled by junior staff officers and by civilian employees of CIFA which, at the time, was the DoD entity overseeing Polygraph Headquarters.

At the same time the memos banned CVSA®, they had the impact of putting American Soldiers in the uncomfortable position of having to ignore existing Army policies found in two Army Field Manuals.

Army Field Manual 2-22.3, Human Intelligence Collector Operations[81], dated September 2006, appears to specifically call for the use of CVSA® by U.S. Army HUMINT collectors. Paragraph 13-7 of the field manual states: "Biometric devices such as voice stress analyzer and polygraph support the determination of the truthfulness of a source."

The paragraph goes on to state that, "The polygraph is of limited usefulness in general HUMINT collection due to the level of expertise needed to operate it and the lack of general availability of the device to the field."

Another Army field manual, AFM 3-24 (MCWP 3-33.5) COUNTERINSURGENCY[82], specifically calls for "collection of personal and biometric data and a search through available reporting databases to determine whether the person is an insurgent" and notes that biometrics concerns the measurement and analysis of unique physical or behavioral characteristics, such as fingerprint or voice patterns.

Dated December 2006, AFM 3-24 was authored by General David Petraeus, the man famous for leading U.S. war efforts in Iraq and Afghanistan before a sex scandal forced him to resigning in disgrace from his position as Director of the Central Intelligence Agency (CIA).

Was CVSA® singled out for exclusion by DoD officials, because it represents the single most-effective challenger to the polygraph? Seems that way.

# CHAPTER TWENTY:
# Singled Out

Since 2008, a number of reports have been produced by a variety of governmental and nongovernmental entities. While some have focused on the situation involving detainees at GITMO, others looked at the progress -- or lack thereof -- being made in the war in Afghanistan. From among the reports available, three warrant special attention.

Amidst media-flamed fires of concern regarding allegations GITMO detainees were being mistreated, members of the U.S. Senate Armed Services Committee (SASC) took steps in 2008 to make them appear proactive as the war approached its seven-year mark.

In addition to holding hearings, they deployed a team of investigators to look into allegations of torture being inflicted upon detainees at GITMO and at other detention facilities in Iraq (i.e., Abu Ghraib, Camp Cropper and Camp Bucca). The investigation resulted in the publication of an unclassified 263-page report, "INQUIRY INTO THE TREATMENT OF DETAINEES IN U.S. CUSTODY,"[83] dated November 20, 2008.

Over the course of their investigation, according to the report, the committee reviewed more than 200,000 pages of classified and unclassified documents, including detention and interrogation policies, memoranda, electronic communications,

217

training manuals and the results of previous investigations into detainee abuse. While the majority of those documents were provided to the committee by DoD, the committee also reviewed documents provided by the DoJ, documents in the public domain, a small number of documents provided by individuals and a number of published secondary sources including books and articles in popular magazines and scholarly journals.

In addition, according to the report, the committee interviewed more than 70 individuals in connection with its inquiry. Most were current or former DoD employees, and some came from the current and former ranks of the Department of Justice, including the FBI.

The committee issued subpoenas, heard testimony from subpoenaed witnesses, sent written questions to more than 200 individuals, and held public hearings June 17 and September 25, 2008.

Though one might have expected to see several mentions of it, since it is *the* only approved credibility-assessment tool for use within DoD, the SASC report included only one mention of the word, polygraph. It appeared in a heavily-redacted paragraph in which interrogators and analysts were said to have attributed the cooperation of one detainee, Mohammed al-Khatani, to several factors, one of which was "his failing a polygraph test."

Only one detainee cooperated.

The report also included mentions of interrogation techniques that were part of the curriculum at U.S. Military Survival Evasion Resistance and Escape (SERE) schools and other non-polygraph interrogation techniques that had been authorized by U.S. Joint Forces Command for use during the interrogation of detainees in U.S. military custody by members of a Joint Personnel Recovery Agency (JPRA) team deployed to Iraq in September 2003.

Most remarkable about the committee's findings, however, were the things not mentioned.

The committee's report failed to mention CVSA® technology and the fact that it had been used successfully to interrogate detainees at GITMO, to interrogate members of the Deck of Cards in Iraq, and to interrogate a diverse range of subjects at locations around the world.

Likewise, it failed to include a single mention of CVSA® or anyone remotely related to it.

As a result of the omissions, the polygraph's leading challenger would remain unknown to anyone relying solely upon the SASC investigators' report for information upon which to make critical decisions.

Almost 30 months after the SASC report, behavioral scientist Jeffrey Bordin, Ph.D., published "A CRISIS OF TRUST AND CULTURAL INCOMPATIBILITY,"[84] a 70-page report focused on the Green-on-Blue/Insider Attack phenomena in Afghanistan.

Commissioned by ISAF leaders, Dr. Bordin's report used "tough love" language -- "this problem is of our own making," "own worst enemy," and "self-defeating" -- to describe ISAF behaviors, policies and decision-making in Afghanistan. In addition, it included more than a half-dozen mentions of the need for improved vetting of Afghans.

Before he was done, Dr. Bordin also included a call to action that seemed to be aimed at the very people who had commissioned his work.

"Four years ago after the May 6, 2007 murder of two U.S. Soldiers (COL James Harrison, Jr., and MSG Wilberto Sabalu, Jr.) by an Afghan National Army (ANA) soldier, an Afghan government official urged 'patience' regarding ISAF's response to this killing. After an additional 54 murders of ISAF personnel since then the time for 'patience' is long past. Decisive actions in countering this murder epidemic are called for."

Couple his call for improved vetting with his declaration that decisive actions are needed, and one might reach the conclusion Dr. Bordin was making a case for CVSA®.

Nineteen months after Dr. Bordin's report was published, Secretary of Defense Leon Panetta showed he really knows how to play politics. His "gamesmanship" surfaced in the form of a 172-page document, "Report on Progress Toward Security and Stability in Afghanistan,"[85] released December 10, 2012.

A DoD news release[86] issued the same day served as confirmation Secretary Panetta was trying to shape the American public's perceptions about Afghanistan. Though Section 1230 of the National Defense Authorization Act for Fiscal Year 2008 (Public Law 110-181) required the Defense boss to release his report in October, no one in Washington, D.C., had wanted more bad news about Green-on-Blue/Insider Attacks to surface so close to Election Day; hence, the reason no one batted an eye when the report was released 34 days late.

Beyond politics, the Executive Summary of Secretary Panetta's report began with a paragraph in which he placed emphasis on squeezing as many "positives" as possible -- some believable, others not -- out of an otherwise-bleak situation.

"During the reporting period of April 1 to September 30, 2012, the Coalition and our Afghan partners blunted the insurgent summer offensive, continued to transition the Afghan National Security Forces (ANSF) into security lead, pushed violence out of most populated areas, and coalition member nations signed several international agreements to support the long-term stability and security of Afghanistan."

It was followed by a paragraph within which three words -- up, down, and disproportionate -- were used in succession to describe the frequency and locations of enemy-initiated attacks (EIAs) during the six-month period.

Secretary Panetta devoted the third paragraph to an explanation about "security progress and the development of the ANSF" going well as the transition toward Afghan control continued.

It wasn't until the fourth paragraph, however, that he began tackling the difficult topic of Green-on-Blue/Insider Attacks.

"The rise in insider attacks has the potential to adversely affect the Coalition's political landscape, but mitigation policies and a collective ISAF-ANSF approach are helping to reduce risks to coalition personnel, and to sustain confidence in the campaign," Secretary Panetta reported. "The cause of and eventual solution to this joint ISAF and ANSF problem will require continuous assessment; it remains clear that the insider threat is both an enemy tactic and has a cultural component."

A master of the obvious, Secretary Panetta went on to report "many mitigation policies recently put in place will require additional time to assess their effects."

More time.

Like Dr. Bordin before him, Secretary Panetta also dedicated space in his report to an explanation of how time ran out for several dozen people -- many of whom were Americans -- who had fallen victim to Green-on-Blue/Insider Attacks.

"Between May 2007 and the end of September 2012," he began, "a total of 79 Insider Attacks occurred. Of those 79 incidents, five (six percent) are possibly or likely attributable to infiltration; 11 (14 percent) are assessed as likely or possibly attributable to co-option; 30 (38 percent) are possibly or likely attributable to personal motives; three (four percent) are considered related to unknown reasons but having insurgent ties, and 30 (38 percent) to unknown (or pending due to ongoing investigations).

"Of the 79 insider attacks," he continued, "69 resulted in CF (military and civilian personnel) deaths and/or wounded, causing a total of 116 CF deaths and 164 CF wounded. As of the end of the reporting period, there have been 37 attacks in 2012, resulting in 51 coalition deaths (32 U.S deaths) and 74 wounded." *NOTE: The report included a footnote about the number of "Green-on-Blue/Insider Attacks" being subject to change based on on-going analysis and reports of new incidents emerging.*

Also like Dr. Bordin, Secretary Panetta addressed the issue of vetting Afghans. In fact, he devoted a full paragraph of his report to the existing eight-step process used to vet Afghans and included a colorful graphic to boot. He did not, however, go so far as to acknowledge that the eight-step vetting process does not work or issue a call for the rapid deployment of something better.

Not unexpectedly, Secretary Panetta made no mention of CVSA® -- especially not as a tool for screening Afghans -- in his report. Instead, he allowed his polygraph-loyalist colors to show.

"ISAF is exploring additional CI initiatives with the ANSF," the report explained, adding that one of the initiatives involves "while expediting CI equipment requirements, e.g., mobile polygraph kits."

Because no fewer than three high-ranking DoD officials had already declared PCASS the only credibility-assessment technology authorized for use within DoD, Secretary Panetta's statement about mobile polygraph kits can only be interpreted in one of two ways: either ANSF units *might be* supplied with PCASS soon or they *will be* supplied with PCASS soon.

Those interpretations beg the question, "If, indeed, PCASS is the best credibility-assessment tool available, then why has it taken so long, at the cost of so many lives, to reach this point?"

It's a question to which several possible answers exist.

Perhaps, Afghan government officials are not interested in using the portable polygraph, because they are keenly aware that it can be defeated by a host of countermeasures.

It could be that officials at the U.S. Department of Commerce are putting a stop to the idea, because federal law prohibits the sale of PCASS to foreign governments.

The most likely answer, however, is that ISAF commanders are not willing to bet their lives, and the lives of their men, on the findings of PCASS exams administered to Afghans.

Barely three months after Secretary Panetta's annual report went public, GAO officials released the agency's own status report[87] about Afghanistan. Not surprisingly, the 59-page report's "key findings" were more grim than those offered in the politically-influenced Defense Secretary's report. Shown below, they need no explanation:

The security situation in Afghanistan, as measured by enemy-initiated attacks, has deteriorated since 2005, affecting

223

U.S. and allied reconstruction operations. DOD attack data as of December 2012 show that the pattern of enemy-initiated attacks has remained seasonal in nature, generally peaking from June through September each year and then declining during the winter months.

Insider attacks on U.S. and coalition military personnel have increased, raising questions about efforts to protect U.S. personnel working with ANSF. One of the central tenets of the NATO-led International Security Assistance Force (ISAF) mission in Afghanistan is enhanced unit partnering in which coalition units provide training, assistance, and development functions to ANSF units until they are able to conduct operations independently. However, between 2007 and 2012, ANSF killed or wounded over 290 U.S. and international coalition personnel in 87 attacks. The number of these attacks has increased over time. Among the attacks with identified causes, DOD and NATO have identified the personal motivations of individual ANSF members—including stress and ideological beliefs of attackers with no previous ties to insurgents—as the largest single cause of insider attacks. According to one ISAF and several DOD officials, as the United States and ISAF continue to shift their focus from a combat to an all advise-and-assist mission, larger numbers of personnel may be exposed to a possible insider attack.

# CHAPTER TWENTY-ONE:
## Hearing Voices

If, as polygraph loyalists have claimed for decades, it is not possible to detect stress in the human voice, then why have so many taxpayer dollars been dedicated to pairing the study of the human voice with credibility-assessment technologies?

Seeking an answer to that question, I contacted Jay F. Nunamaker, Ph.D. and lead researcher at the National Center for Border Security and Immigration[88] (a.k.a., "BORDERS") at the University of Arizona in Tucson. In reply to my inquiry August 6, 2012, Dr. Nunamaker shared details about the project.

He began by explaining that the program has received funding from several sources, including -- but not limited to -- the U.S. Department of Homeland Security (DHS), the Intelligence Advanced Research Projects Activity (IARPA), the National Science Foundation (NSF), and no fewer than three branches of the U.S. military.

Next, he described the history of the project.

"We started down this path to develop a non-intrusive, non-invasive next-generation polygraph about 10 years ago with funding from the Polygraph Institute at Ft. Jackson," he wrote.

Ten years?

If, per Dr. Nunamaker, the effort began 10 years ago at Polygraph Headquarters, that means it got its start at about the same time the NRC report[89] was published and offered, among other things, that the majority of 57 research studies touted by APA were "unreliable, unscientific and biased."

In a message August 31, 2012, Dr. Nunamaker offered more details about his research.

"The UA team has created an Automated Virtual Agent for Truth Assessment in Real-Time (AVATAR) that uses an embodied conversational agent--an animated human face backed by biometric sensors and intelligent agents--to conduct interviews," he explained. "It is currently being used at the Nogales Mexico-U.S. border and is designed to detect changes in arousal, behavior and cognitive effort that may signal stress, risk or credibility."

In the same message, Dr. Nunamaker pointed me to a then-recent article[90] in which the AVATAR system was described as one that uses "speech recognition and voice-anomaly-detection software" to flag certain exchanges "as questionable and worthy of follow-up interrogation."

Those exchanges, according to the article, "are color coded green, yellow or red to highlight the potential severity of questionable responses." Ring familiar?

Further into the article, reporter Larry Greenemeier relied upon Aaron Elkins, a post-doctoral researcher who helped develop the system, to provide an explanation of how anomaly detection is employed by AVATAR.

After stating that it is based on vocal characteristics, Elkins explained a number of ways in which a person's voice might tip the program. One of his explanations was particularly interesting.

"The kiosk's speech recognition software monitors the content of an interviewee's answers and can flag a response indicating when, for example, a person acknowledges having a criminal record."

Elkins clarified his views further during an interview[91] eight days later.

"I will stress that is a very large leap to say that they're lying...or what they're saying is untrue -- but what it does is draw attention that there is something going on," he said. At the end of that statement, reporter Som Lisaius added seven words -- *precisely the intent behind any credibility assessment* -- with which I'm certain every CVSA® examiner I've interviews during the past four years would agree.

To even the most-impartial observer, Elkins' explanations confirm beyond a shadow of a doubt that BORDERS researchers believe stress can be detected in the voice utterances of individuals facing real-life jeopardy.

NOTE: Though I tried twice between August 2012 and February 2013 to find out from officials at the BORDERS program how much funding they have received from the U.S. Department of Homeland Security and all other sources since the inception of the program, I received no replies to my inquiries.

# CHAPTER TWENTY-TWO:
# The Capstone

Twenty-four-hundred miles east of Tucson, a man in Upstate New York spent more than four decades believing stress can be detected in the voice utterances of individuals facing real-life jeopardy.

Not your stereotypical academic, Professor Emeritus James L. Chapman began his adult life as a United States Marine and served in Southeast Asia. From there, he went on to become a New York cop and, later, a criminology justice and forensic crime professor at the State University of New York. And, oh yes, he's the same professor I mentioned as having contacted Professor Damphousse and the other researchers involved in The Oklahoma Study.

When he wasn't teaching, Professor Chapman helped law enforcement professionals across the nation use CVSA® as an investigative tool.

During Professor Chapman's four decades of work in the field of credibility assessment, he conducted more than 15,000 exams, ascended to the level of Master CVSA® examiner, served as director of Standards and Training of the National Association of Computer Voice Stress Analysts (NACVSA)[92], and built a reputation as the world's foremost authority on the application of CVSA® as an investigative tool.

After retiring from full-time teaching, Professor Chapman refocused his efforts on finding a more global way to disseminate the positive findings he had gathered on the use of CVSA®. Although he wrote a lengthy white paper detailing his data and results, his ultimate mission was to publish the latter in a peer-reviewed, criminology-based scientific journal.

In June 2010, Professor Chapman teamed up with Marigo Stathis, hoping she could help him reach the goal he had previously been unable to reach on his own.

Stathis, a well-respected neuroscientist and research analyst, brought to the equation her in-depth knowledge of the scientific method, statistics, and academic research experience that includes authorship of 27 published scientific articles.

Before working together, both Professor Chapman and Stathis discussed the obstacles each foresaw regarding their collaboration and the creation of a manuscript worthy of publication.

Professor Chapman warned Stathis of the turf war between polygraph loyalists and others advocating the use of other credibility-assessment technologies, including CVSA®. In turn, Stathis reassured the professor that the statistical analyses and numbers would hold their own and reveal the "truth" of the matter if CVSA® was truly as effective as he claimed.

Stathis also made it clear that, as a scientist, her goal was not to disprove other technologies (of which she had no prior knowledge or bias), but to illuminate and showcase Professor Chapman's particular study of CVSA®. In addition, she reiterated that a scientific study worthy of publication should present hypotheses, methodologies, data, results, and conclusions that stand on their own merits.

After six months of intense collaboration which included consultations with world-class statisticians at The Johns

Hopkins University, Professor Chapman and Stathis completed the first version of their paper showcasing the CVSA®-focused research study. After choosing a few reputable criminology-oriented, scientific journals in North America, they submitted the paper to the first, hopeful for a positive response. Soon thereafter, they received their first rejection letter. Still hopeful, however, they used the criticisms they received to rewrite the paper, and submitted it to their second choice journal. A few months later, they received the reply: another rejection letter.

A few months later, however, they received the reply: a rejection letter.

Although disappointed, Professor Chapman was not surprised. He had, after all, witnessed the turf war firsthand.

Stathis was surprised, but undaunted, having amassed considerable experience when it came to editorial peer reviews and publications. She was familiar with rejection and understood that rewriting a paper based on reviewers' comments and suggestions only makes for a stronger end product.

Despite the level of harshness, the types of editorial criticism to which she was accustomed were always grounded in validity and solid reasoning. Conversely, she was taken aback by some of what she perceived to be illogical, inaccurate, and even emotional feedback about the paper she and Professor Chapman had submitted.

One journal reviewer cited the studies completed by researchers at the universities in Florida and Oklahoma as reasons to discount the CVSA® study, apparently not realizing they had already been debunked.

Another cited the lack of laboratory studies to prove the technology works, despite the fact that Professor Chapman's study was clearly cited as a "field-based" one, requiring real-world settings where jeopardy is present.

Still another reviewer, obviously not aware of the research being done in Arizona, claimed there was little or no scientific basis for claims that voice stress can be measured.

Due to their shared conviction in the validity and worth of the study, however, Professor Chapman and Stathis decided to remain persistent despite the opposition. After several months of further rewriting and chiseling, the duo finalized the last version of their manuscript in March 2012 and submitted it for peer review to editors at *Criminalistics and Court Expertise*, one of the world's oldest and most-reputable scientific journals.

Although nervous about the fate of the paper, Professor Chapman and Stathis knew their final manuscript was scientifically sound. Every "i" was dotted, and every "t" was crossed. Several more months passed as the peer-review process took place. Then, finally, the pair's efforts culminated in acceptance. Their paper, "A Long-Term, Retrospective Field Evaluation Of Voice Stress Analysis In A Criminal Justice Setting,"[93] was published in the journal's December 2012 edition.

Unfortunately, Professor Chapman passed away unexpectedly at the age of 69, one month after the paper had been submitted for peer review, and never got to see it published. Others, however, will see the paper and learn from it, a capstone on the professor's long and distinguished career.

The retrospective field study was, according to its authors, based upon actual CVSA® examinations Professor Chapman conducted in the United States and Canada during an 18-year period. It involved conducting four extremely thorough statistical analyses of data related to actual criminal cases, suspects and persons of interest. No white coats or lab rats were involved.

The total inventory of cases submitted was culled for ones that met several key criteria: A) A confession was a potential outcome; B) There was no involvement with veracity testing of previous statements; C) No employment clearance was involved; D) The case was not used as confirmation of prior witness testimony; and E) The facts of the case were such that responses could be verified by means of structured CVSA® follow-up questioning.

After excluding cases that did not meet all of the above criteria, the number of criminal cases remaining for study totaled 2,109. Those cases were then numbered in consecutive order, and 236 cases for study were randomly selected, by chance, from that number.

The cases selected involved 329 specific crimes, including -- but not limited to -- multiple homicides, corporate theft, organized crime, contract murders, sexual abuse of children and arson for hire.

Subjects examined represented a wide spectrum of people, male and female, and included individuals with no criminal history as well as others with arrest and/or conviction records.

The socio-economic strata ran the gamut from wealthy, well-educated professionals to illiterate indigents and included several subjects who had been professionally evaluated and found to be of below-normal intelligence.

The livelihoods of those within the study group ranged from elected public officials to professional criminals and even included some organized crime "hit men."

Of the cases studied, according to the study's final report, 91 percent represented criminal investigations in which legal authorities had reached investigative impasses. In other words, after following standard investigative protocols, investigators had been unable to reach firm conclusions as to the guilt or innocence of the subjects.

Each subject named in the "Confession Possibility List" was individually interviewed by the CVSA® examiner with two goals in mind: (1) To exonerate the innocent and identify the guilty, and (2) To obtain legally-valid and independently-verifiable confessions from those subjects who were unable to clear the CVSA® process.

Each interview, according to the final report, was conducted according to a standard protocol in which the wording of the interview, but not the methodology, was adapted on site to the specifics of each case.

In each case, the procedure used by the CVSA® researcher consisted of six steps:

Step 1 -- The CVSA® examiner was briefed by the requesting authorities in order to become familiar with the circumstances of each case. This briefing included available physical evidence, witness and suspect statements collected to date, and any background information concerning the subject to be tested. A determination of focus areas for questioning was made at that time by the CVSA® examiner.

Step 2 -- A recorded pre-test interview with the subject was conducted. Also, during this portion of the interview, sufficient time was allotted to: a) obtain the subject's informed consent for the interview; b) review the topical areas of questioning with the subject; c) attempt to help the subject relax and feel at ease with the examiner; d) provide an opportunity to discuss the subject's concerns and to clarify terms and issues; and e) allow the examiner to formulate precise questions to be asked of the subject during the CVSA® examination.

Step 3 -- The initial test questions were then presented to the subject. Examinations contained from nine to 31 questions, consisting of relevant, irrelevant, and control questions for which the subject provided "yes" or "no" answers. The initial set of questions was designed to address specific issues concerning the crime(s). As the examination progressed, the questions became more specific about the crime issue(s). Included in the set of questions, interspersed among the relevant questions, were questions with known answers, such as, *"Is your name Bob Smith?"* To this, the subject was directed to answer correctly. Other questions with known answers were also included, but to which the subject was directed to answer incorrectly. The CVSA® graphs produced by these non-relevant questions provide the examiner with additional reference points for the interpretation of the CVSA® results.

Step 4 -- The fourth step included processing the responses with the CVSA® instrument, after which the resulting CVSA® charts were analyzed and interpreted by the examiner.

Step 5 -- If stress patterns associated with specific relevant questions were observed by the examiner, an opportunity was given for the subject to provide additional clarification regarding the stress. Prior to the re-examination, questions were reformulated by the examiner to evaluate the veracity of the explanations offered by the subject. This procedure was repeated until all necessary questions had received responses that included no displays of stress reaction, or until the remaining stress reactions could not be eliminated by the explanation or the re-questioning.

Step 6 -- The final step of the process was to provide a conclusion regarding the outcome of the CVSA® examination. If the relevant questions produced a "No Stress" chart, the subject was "cleared" by the CVSA® procedure. This information was then turned over to the agency requesting the examination.

If a confession was made by the subject during the CVSA® examination, the examiner would ask the subject to support his/her confession by verifying details or by providing further details concerning the events under investigation. Further, if a confession occurred, the subject was asked to provide a written statement and to confirm evidence that had not been made public about the case. Another CVSA® examination would then be conducted to validate the accuracy of the written statement. If no confession occurred, the examiner reported the findings to the agency requesting the CVSA® examination, such that the information could guide further investigation.

Of the 329 confession possibilities in this study, 92.1 percent of the CVSA® examinations produced a "Stress Indicated" result and 89 percent of those culminated in actual confessions. Most notably, suspects made self-incriminating confessions during 96.4 percent of the interviews during which CVSA® indicated stress.

The results of this study, according to its authors, clearly demonstrate CVSA® is not only a useful tool in obtaining valid confessions, but also that the likelihood of obtaining valid confessions increases based upon whether or not stress is present for relevant crime issues.

In each of the 236 cases included in the study, inclusive of 329 confession possibilities, a trained and experienced CVSA® examiner (i.e., Professor Chapman) used well-established CVSA® protocols with the objectives of producing legally-admissible confessions and obtaining additional supporting evidence from suspects and/or persons of interest.

With current scientific research revealing that only 20 percent to 50 percent of police interviews/interrogations produce valid confessions, the study's authors explained, a 96.4 percent-verified confession rate is considered phenomenally high.

Adding to the conclusions above, the study's authors shared additional findings.

"More importantly," they wrote, "this study also proves CVSA® to be a useful and predictive tool in separating the innocent from the guilty, by conclusively demonstrating the ability to discriminate stress from no-stress in the human voice. In one stand-alone case of Grand Larceny, 20 individuals were considered suspects. Of the 20 CVSA® examinations conducted for this case, 19 resulted in a finding of 'No Stress Indicated,' while only one produced a 'Stress Indicated' finding – resulting in a confession.

By use of the CVSA®, the accurate identification/ separation of the 19 innocent individuals from the one who was guilty, far surpassed a "chance" rate of accuracy. The probability of 20 successful evaluations would have been less than 1 in 1,000,000."

In summary, the conclusions of the study were: (1) During criminal justice investigations, CVSA® can serve as a reliable decision support tool to help discriminate between "Deception" and "No Deception"; (2) Voice stress and confession rates are interdependent; (3) The CVSA® process can precisely and accurately discriminate stress from no stress in real-life crime situations involving consequence and jeopardy; and (4) the level of consequence and jeopardy associated with specific crimes can affect the confession rates obtained from guilty individuals under examination.

In January 2013, Stathis shared the results of the study with attendees at a worldwide conference of CVSA® examiners held in South Florida. In addition to highlighting the information outlined above, Stathis delivered a clear message to those who discount the technology proven to work by Professor Chapman.

"Just as you would not call an X-ray scan a prop if it provides accurate information that helps a medical doctor in formulating a diagnosis," she said, "you would not call the CVSA chart a prop if it reveals accurate information that helps a trained detective in making an assessment. The CVSA is not a prop. It's a tool."

# EPILOGUE

On Saturday, June 19, 2010, Reuters[94] cited a Saudi security official as saying around 25 former GITMO detainees had returned to militancy after going through a so-called "rehabilitation" program for Al-Qaeda members. Considering the source of that information, one can safely conclude that the actual number is probably higher. At the same time, one might draw more from the content of the article.

First, one might conclude that the number of detainees returning to militancy could have been reduced *if* interrogators at GITMO and at similar detention facilities around the world had been allowed to continue using CVSA® as an interrogation tool for determining which detainees, among those being held, were being deceptive about their future plans.

Second, one might conclude that the number of American and coalition personnel killed and wounded in Green-on-Blue/Insider Attacks in Afghanistan could have been reduced substantially *if* our warfighters had been allowed to continue using CVSA® to interrogate enemy combatants as well as others suspected of waging war against us and those wanting to work alongside our warfighters.

Unfortunately, CVSA® remains banned from use within DoD as this book was going to press, the eight-step vetting process continues to be used to vet Afghans, and many if-then questions remain unanswered for loved ones of those killed and wounded during Green-on-Blue/Insider Attacks.

If CVSA® is good enough to be relied upon by investigators at more than 1,800 local, state and federal law enforcement agencies across the United States, then why isn't it good enough for DoD?

If CVSA® is good enough to be relied upon by officials inside some 200 foreign government agencies and, unlike PCASS, can be exported overseas with approval from the U.S. Department of Commerce, then why isn't it good enough for DoD?

If CVSA® is good enough to have earned the approval of a U.S. federal court judge, then why isn't it good enough for DoD?

If CVSA® is good enough to have survived an in-depth peer-review process conducted by officials at one of the world's premier scientific journals, then why isn't it good enough for DoD?

Our nation's civilian and military leaders must take steps immediately to end the turf war between polygraph loyalists and their challengers!

It's time to rescind all directives and memos banning CVSA® within DoD so that warfighters and others supporting the war effort will be able to select the tool they deem best for the job at hand.

It's time to reconsider whether to allow our military and intelligence professionals to continue using the polygraph and the PCASS, especially in situations where American lives are at stake.

It's time to allow U.S. military and intelligence professionals to use whatever credibility-assessment tools they believe are best suited for the task at hand -- even if they choose CVSA®.

There's no reason why DoD should continue to ban CVSA®. If they do maintain the ban, they need to explain why -- *and NOW!*

This story is far from over.

# ACKNOWLEDGEMENTS

I send special thanks to my wife and sons for continuing to put up with my writing obsession. Thanks also to those individuals who offered encouragement and eyeballs to this effort at various points along the way. Too numerous to name, you know who you are.

# ABOUT THE AUTHOR

A native of Enid, Oklahoma, Bob McCarty graduated from Oklahoma State University with a degree in journalism in 1984. During the next 20 years, he served stints as an Air Force public affairs officer, a political campaign manager, a technology sales consultant and a corporate public relations professional.

In October 2006, Bob began writing full time at BobMcCarty.com.

In October 2011, he published his first nonfiction book, Three Days In August: A U.S. Army Special Forces Soldier's Fight For Military Justice, which chronicles the life and wrongful conviction of Green Beret Sergeant First Class Kelly A. Stewart.

Along with his wife, three tall sons and two short cats, Bob lives near St. Louis, Missouri.

CONNECT ONLINE
http://TheClapperMemo.com
http://BobMcCarty.com

# GLOSSARY

| | |
|---|---|
| AAFES | Army and Air Force Exchange Service |
| AAR | After Action Review or After Action Report |
| ABA | American Bar Association |
| ADAM | Arrestee Drug Abuse Monitoring |
| ADDT | Alternate Detection of Deception Technology |
| AFOSI | Air Force Office of Special Investigations |
| ALP | Afghan Local Police |
| ANA | Afghan National Army |
| ANSF | Afghan National Security Force |
| APA | American Polygraph Association |
| ASC | American Society of Criminology |
| ASG | Afghan Security Group |
| ASIS | American Society of Industrial Security |
| AU | University of Arizona |
| AVATAR | Automated Virtual Agent for Truth Assessment in Real-Time |
| CALL | Army Centers for Army Lessons Learned |
| CENTCOM | U.S. Central Command |
| CF | Coalition Forces |
| CI | Counterintelligence |
| CIA | Central Intelligence Agency |
| CIFA | Counterintelligence Field Activity |
| CV | Curriculum vitae |
| CVSA® | Computer Voice Stress Analyzer®[95] |
| DACA | Defense Academy for Credibility Assessment |
| DACP | Defense Acquisition Challenge Program |

| | |
|---|---|
| DARPA | Defense Advanced Research Projects Agency |
| DCIS | Defense Criminal Investigative Service |
| DDI | Director of Defense Intelligence |
| DHS | Department of Homeland Security |
| DI | Deception Indicated (Polygraph) |
| DIA | Defense Intelligence Agency |
| DNI | Director of National Intelligence |
| DoD | Department of Defense |
| DoDPI | Department of Defense Polygraph Institute |
| DoJ | Department of Justice |
| DSD | Deputy Secretary of Defense |
| DSS | Defense Security Service |
| DUSD | Deputy Under Secretary of Defense |
| EIA | Enemy-Initiated Attack |
| FIST | Field Interrogation Support Tool |
| FOIA | Freedom of Information Act |
| FOB | Forward Operating Base |
| GAO | U.S. Government Accountability Office |
| GIRoA | Government of the Islamic Republic of Afghanistan |
| GMS | Grant Management System (NIJ) |
| GTMO | U.S. Naval Station Guantanamo (a.k.a., "GITMO") |
| HUMINT | Human Intelligence |
| IACP | International Association of Chiefs of Police |
| IARPA | Intelligence Advanced Research Projects Activity |
| ICE | Interrogation Control Element |
| IED | Improvised Explosive Device |
| IRB | Institutional Review Board |
| ISAF | International Security Assistance Force |

| | |
|---|---|
| ISOF | Iraqi Special Operations Forces |
| JPRA | Joint Personnel Recovery Agency |
| JTF-GTMO | Joint Task Force Guantanamo |
| KayTen | Kayten Research and Development, L.L.C. |
| LEAF | Northeast Law Enforcement Analysis Facility |
| LLC | Limited-Liability Company |
| LVA | Layered-Voice Analysis |
| MoD | Ministry of Defense (Afghanistan) |
| MoI | Ministry of Interior (Afghanistan) |
| NACVSA | National Association of Computer Voice Stress Analysts |
| NAS | National Academic of Sciences |
| NATO | North Atlantic Treaty Organization |
| NCCA | National Center for Credibility Assessment |
| NDI | No Deception Indicated (Polygraph) |
| NDS | National Directorate of Security (Afghanistan) |
| NGA | National Geospatial-Intelligence Agency |
| NIJ | National Institute of Justice |
| NIMA | National Imagery and Mapping Agency |
| NITV | National Institute for Truth Verification |
| NO | No Opinion (Polygraph) |
| NRC | National Research Council |
| NRO | National Reconnaissance Office |
| NSF | National Science Foundation |
| OCOM | Office of Communications (NIJ) |
| ODMHSAS | Oklahoma Dept. of Mental Health & Substance Abuse Services |
| ODNI | Office of the Director of National Intelligence |
| OSoS | Oklahoma Secretary of State |
| OS&T | Office of Science & Technology (NIJ) |
| PAO | Public Affairs Officer |

| | |
|---|---|
| PCASS | Portable or Preliminary Credibility Assessment Screening System |
| PSC | Private Security Company |
| PDA | Personal Digital Assistant |
| PoP | Proof of Principle Testing |
| QRF | Quick Reaction Force |
| R/IST | Relevant/Irrelevant Screening Tests |
| SASC | Senate Armed Services Committee |
| SERE | Survival Evasion Resistance and Escape |
| SF | Special Forces |
| SFG | Special Forces Group |
| SHA | Sullivan Haave Associates |
| SOCOM | U.S. Special Operations Command |
| TCN | Third-Country National |
| TOC | Tactical Operations Center |
| TRADOC | Army Training & Doctrine Command |
| USDCS | Under Secretary of Defense for Counterintelligence and Security |
| USDI | Under Secretary of Defense for Intelligence |
| VSA™ | Voice Stress Analysis™[96] |

[1] Author(s) unknown, "Biography of James R. Clapper, Director of National Intelligence," January 6, 2013, Office of the Director of National Intelligence, Washington, D.C., http://dni.gov/index.php/about/leadership/director-of-national-intelligence.
[2] Blackburn, Bradley. "DNI James Clapper Admits He Was Not Briefed on London Arrests," December 22, 2010, ABC News, http://abcnews.go.com/US/director-national-intelligence-james-clapper-briefed-london-arrests/story?id=12458010.
[3] Author(s) unknown. "DNI James Clapper: Muslim Brotherhood "Largely Secular," "Has Eschewed Violence," February 10, 2011, RealClearPolitics.com. http://www.realclearpolitics.com/video/2011/02/10/dni_james_clapper_muslim_brotherhood_a_largely_secular_group.html.
[4] Tria, Len. "Benghazi fiasco revisited," December 23, 2012, Hernando (Florida) Today/Tampa Bay Online, http://www2.hernandotoday.com/news/opinion/2012/dec/23/haopino1-benghazi-fiasco-revisited-ar-590002/.
[5] Dedman, Bill. "New anti-terror weapon: Hand-held lie detector," MSNBC.com, April 9, 2008, http://msnbc.com/id/23926278.
[6] Author's name redacted, "Army Regulation 15-6 Findings and Recommendations Concerning Hostile Fire Deaths and Injuries, 4th Squadron, 2nd Stryker Cavalry Regiment, Forward Operating Base Frontenac, Afghanistan April 14, 2011," April 14, 2011, U.S. Army.
[7] Author(s) unknown, "NATO Media Backgrounder," March 2011, Public Diplomacy Division (PDD) - Press & Media Section Media Operations Section (MOC), International Security Assistance Force, Kabul Afghanistan, http://www.isaf.nato.int/images/stories/File/factsheets/0423-11_ANSF_LR_en(1).pdf.
[8] "Senate Armed Services Committee Holds Hearing on the Situation in Afghanistan," Transcript of testimony offered by General John R. Allen, International Security Assistance Force commander, before Senate Armed Services Committee, March 22, 2012, Washington, D.C. See also: http://youtu.be/_Ic8p8Lup6w.
[9] Druzin, Heath. "Five U.S. Troops Wounded in Latest 'Green-on-Blue'

251

Attack in Afghanistan," July 4, 2012, Stars and Stripes, http://www.stripes.com/news/five-us-troops-wounded-in-latest-green-on-blue-attack-in-afghanistan-1.182061.

[10] Shaughnessy, Larry. "Pentagon Changing Lingo for Growing Threat in Afghanistan," August 14, 2012, CNN, http://security.blogs.cnn.com/2012/08/14/pentagon-changing-lingo-for-growing-threat-in-afghanistan/.

[11] Lerman, David and Lakshmanan, Indira A. R. "Most 'Insider Attacks' Aren't Taliban,' Pentagon Says," August 20, 2012, Bloomberg.com, http://www.bloomberg.com/news/2012-08-20/most-afghan-insider-attacks-aren-t-taliban-pentagon-says.html.

[12] Wendle, John. "Unfriendly Fire: Can the U.S. and NATO Prevent 'Green-on-Blue' Attacks in Afghanistan," TIME/World, September 4, 2012, http://world.time.com/2012/09/04/unfriendly-fire-can-the-u-s-and-nato-prevent-green-on-blue-attacks-in-afghanistan/.

[13] Committee to Review the Scientific Evidence on the Polygraph, "The Polygraph and Lie Detection," 2003, National Research Council, Washington, D.C.

[14] Bell, Allan D., Jr. "The PSE: A Decade of Controversy," March 1981, Security Management, American Society of Industrial Security, Alexandria, Virginia, http://ASISonline.org.

[15] Author(s) unknown, "The Origin and Evolution of NCCA," Publication Date Unknown, National Center for Credibility Assessment, Fort Jackson, South Carolina, http://ncca.mil/history.

[16] Author(s) unknown. "Department of Defense POLYGRAPH PROGRAM ANNUAL POLYGRAPH REPORT TO CONGRESS Fiscal Year 2000, Publication Date Unknown, Office of the Assistant Secretary of Defense (Command, Control, Communication, and Intelligence), Washington, D.C., http://fas.org/sgp/othergov/polygraph/dod-2000.html.

[17] Author(s) unknown. "Department of Defense Polygraph Program Process and Compliance Study," December 19, 2011, Northrop Grumman/TASC, Inc./Six3Systems, Inc., per contract HQ0034-07-A-1040-0016, Office of the Under Secretary of Defense for Intelligence, Washington, D.C.

[18] Webb, Milton O. "President's Message," MARCH/APRIL 2002, APA Newsletter, American Polygraph Association.

[19] Krapohl, Donald J., Ryan, Andrew H. Jr., and Shull, Kendall W. "Voice stress devices and the detection of lies," 2002, Policy Review, International Chiefs of Police Law Enforcement Policy Center.
[20] Committee to Review the Scientific Evidence on the Polygraph, "The Polygraph and Lie Detection," 2002, National Research Council, Washington, D.C.
[21] Internic.org is a website, operated by the Internet Corporation for Assigned Names and Numbers (ICANN), via which one can learn the identity of a person or group who registers a domain name, http://reports.internic.net/cgi/whois?whois_nic=voicestress.org&type=domain.
[22] Senter, Stuart, Waller, James, and Krapohl, Donald. "Validation Studies for the Preliminary Credibility Assessment Screening System (PCASS)," November 2006, Department of Defense Polygraph Institute, Fort Jackson, South Carolina.
[23] Author(s)/Producer(s) unknown, "Raw Video: Kidnapping by Mexican Police," June 14, 2012, Associated Press, http://youtu.be/cZ-6jNJQeKY.
[24] Stevenson, Mark. "Kidnapping by Mexican police caught on video," June 14, 2012, Associated Press, http://bigstory.ap.org/article/kidnapping-mexican-police-caught-video.
[25] St. Clair, Jeffrey. "Rumsfeld's Enforcer," February 7, 2006, Counterpunch.org, http://www.counterpunch.org/2006/02/07/rumsfeld-s-enforcer.
[26] Mears, Bill. "Deal in Wen Ho Lee case may be imminent," May 22, 2006, CNN, http://www.cnn.com/2006/LAW/05/22/scotus.wenholee.
[27] Gallagher, Gary, Ph.D., et al. "USSOCOM Survey of Law Enforcement End Users of CVSA®," March 2005, U.S. Special Operations Command.
[28] Author(s) unknown. "A family connection: Sullivan Haave may be tiny, but it does have an influential Pentagon link," October 30, 2003, The Center for Public Integrity, http://www.publicintegrity.org/2003/10/30/5637/family-connection.
[29] Hettena, Seth. "Feasting on the Spoils: The Life and Times of Randy "Duke" Cunningham, History's Most Corrupt Congressman," July 10, 2007, St. Martin's Press, http://www.amazon.com/Feasting-Spoils-Cunningham-Historys-Congressman/dp/0312368291/ref=ntt_at_ep_dpt_1.
[30] Author(s) unknown, "TALKING PAPER ON SCREENING TEST FOR

DETAINEE OPERATIONS," October 23, 2006, U.S. Air Force Polygraph Program, http://s3.documentcloud.org/documents/528234/fortishseven.txt.
[31] Damphousse, Kelly R., Ph.D., ""Assessing the Validity of Voice Stress Analysis Tools in a Jail Setting (National Institute of Justice Contract #2005-IJ-CX-0047)," March 31, 2007, Oklahoma Department of Mental Health and Substance Abuse Services, Oklahoma City, Oklahoma.
[32] ADAM is an acronym for the Arrestee Drug Abuse Monitoring model Professor Damphousse used in a previous NIJ-funded study that involved interviewing arrestees about their use of drugs.
[33] Haddad, Darren et al, "INVESTIGATION AND EVALUATION OF VOICE STRESS ANALYSIS TECHNOLOGY, March 20, 2002, National Institute of Justice, U.S. Department of Justice, Washington, D.C.
[34] "LVA" is an acronym for "Layered-Voice Analysis," another voice analysis technology unrelated to the Computer Voice Stress Analyzer® or the National Institute for Truth Verification.
[35] Author(s) unknown, Defense Acquisition Challenge Program Budget Document, February 2005, Department of Defense, Washington, D.C.
[36] Kauchak, Marty. "Defense Acquisition Challenge Program," Special Operations Technology Online Archives (Volume: 3 Issue 5), August 16, 2005.
[37] Hollien, Harry, Ph.D., and Harnsberger, James D., Ph.D. "Voice Stress Analyzer Instrumentation Evaluation (Counterintelligence Field Activity Contract #FA 4814-04-0011)," March 17, 2006, University of Florida, Gainesville, Florida.
[38] Hollrah, Paul R. "Pentagon Obstructionism," September 5, 2006, Townhall.com/The Conservative Voice, http://www.theconservativevoice.com/article/18022.html#.
[39] Ross, Brian, et al. "Innocent Until Proven Guilty," ABC News Primetime, March 30, 2006, http://abcnews.go.com/Primetime/story?id=1786421 &page=2 #.T0PjkszsWkE.
[40] Ross, Brian et al. "Innocent Until Proven Guilty," ABC News Primetime, March 30, 2006, http://abcnews.go.com/Primetime/story?id=1786421& page=2#.T0PjkszsWkE.
[41] Dawn Associates, L.L.C./Slattery Associates, Inc., http://www.polygraphexperts.com/

Bob McCarty

42 John J. Palmatier, Ph.D., http://www.polygraphexperts.com/.
43 Hansen, Mark, "Truth Sleuth or Faulty Detector?" May 1999, ABA JOURNAL, American Bar Association.
44 Greenwald, Glenn. "The unresolved story of ABC News' false Saddam-anthrax report," Salon.com, April 9, 2007, http://www.salon.com/2007/04/09/abc_anthrax/.
45 Cook, John. "America's Wrongest Reporter, ABC News' Brian Ross, Demonstrates Yet Again How He Earned the Title," Gawker.com, July 20, 2012, http://gawker.com/5927715.
46 Author(s) unknown. Profile of Jeff Deskovic case, The Innocence Project/Benjamin N. Cardozo School of Law/Yeshiva University, http://www.innocenceproject.org/Content/Jeff_Deskovic.php.
47 Author(s) unknown. "Geraldo Rivera Live," May 30, 2000, CNN, http://thewebsafe.tripod.com/05302000petrocelliongeraldo.htm.
48 Author(s) unknown. "CNN Newsstand," June 6, 2000, CNN, http://thewebsafe.tripod.com/06062000gelbonnewsstand.htm.
49 Maschke, George W. "Polygraph Operator 'Dr.' Edward I. Gelb Exposed as a Phony Ph.D. Past President of the American Polygraph Association Obtained Degree from an Unaccredited Diploma Mill," June 16, 2003, Antipolygraph.org, http://antipolygraph.org/articles/article-036.shtml.
50 Statement of Robert J. Cramer, U.S. General Accounting Office Managing Director Office of Special Investigations, made during testimony before the U.S. Senate Committee on Governmental Affairs, May 11, 2004, Washington, D.C.
51 Taylor, Marisa, "As polygraph screening flourishes, critics say oversight abandoned," December 6, 2012, McClatchy News, http://www.mcclatchydc.com/2012/12/06/176310/as-polygraph-screening-flourishes.html.
52 News Release, "Director Clapper Announces Steps to Deter and Detect Unauthorized Disclosures," June 25, 2012, Office of the Director of National Intelligence, Washington, D.C., http://dni.gov/index.php/newsroom/press-releases/96-press-releases-2012/586-director-clapper-announces-steps-to-deter-and-detect-unauthorized-disclosures.
53 Porco, Michael V. "Career Highlights" section of Porco Security & Investigative Services website, National Harbor, Maryland,

255

http://porcoinvestigativeservices.com/career-highlights.html.
[54] McParland, Kelly. "Kelly McParlan: Leak machine chugs away on Obama's reputation," August 2, 2012, National Post, http://fullcomment.nationalpost.com/2012/08/02/kelly-mcparland-obama-conveniently-benefits-from-river-of-strategic-leaks/.
[55] Shane, Scott. "Inquiry Into U.S. Leaks Is Casting Chill Over Coverage," August 1, 2012, The New York Times, http://www.nytimes.com/2012/08/02/us/national-security-leaks-lead-to-fbi-hunt-and-news-chill.html.
[56] Halper, Daniel. "Another Leak of Sensitive Intelligence," August 2, 2012, The Weekly Standard, http://www.weeklystandard.com/blogs/another-leak-sensitive-intelligence-information_649237.html.
[57] Taylor, Marisa et al. "The Polygraph Files," July-December 2012, McClatchy News, http://www.mcclatchydc.com/polygraph/.
[58] Taylor, Marisa. "Sen. Charles Grassley seeks probe of polygraph techniques at National Reconnaissance Office," July 27, 2012, McClatchy News, http://www.mcclatchydc.com/2012/07/27/158078/sen-charles-grassley-seeks-probe.html.
[59] Kempster, Norman. "Shultz Says He Will Resign if Ordered to Take Lie Test," December 20, 1985, Los Angeles Times, http://articles.latimes.com/1985-12-20/news/mn-4929_1_lie-detector-test.
[60] Kessler, Ronald. "Spies, Lies, Averted Eyes," March 8, 1994, The New York Times, http://www.nytimes.com/1994/03/08/opinion/spies-lies-averted-eyes.html.
[61] Weiner, Tim. "The C.I.A.'s most Important Mission: Itself," December 10, 1995, The New York Times, http://www.nytimes.com/1995/12/10/magazine/the-cia-s-most-important-mission-itself.html.
[62] Majority opinion written by U.S. Supreme Court Associate Justice Clarence Thomas in U.S. v. Scheffer, March 31, 1998, Cornell University Law School, Ithaca, N.Y., http://chrome.law.cornell.edu/supct/html/96-1133.ZO.html.
[63] Federal Business Opportunities, Ref. Number H9CI0160091, April 10, 2006, https://www.fbo.gov/index?s=opportunity&mode=form&id=67ca1d4da2948ae3e0ed615ef94fc99f&tab=core&tabmode=list&print_preview=1.

[64] Senter, Stuart, Waller, James, and Krapohl, Donald. "Validation Studies for the Preliminary Credibility Assessment Screening System (PCASS)," November 2006, Department of Defense Polygraph Institute, Fort Jackson, South Carolina.

[65] Federal Business Opportunities, Ref. Number H9CI0170093, April 13, 2007, https://www.fbo.gov/index?s=opportunity&mode=form&id=25b688329cb89f a7c403ff254ecca612&tab=core&_cview=0.

[66] Federal Business Opportunities, Ref. Number H9CI0180063, June 18, 2008, https://www.fbo.gov/?s=opportunity&mode=form&id=3e2019e98747f2439e b4107412b9eb0b&tab=core&tabmode=list&print_preview=1.

[67] In the message, Damphousse referred to the American Society of Criminology as "ASC." The presentation to which he referred had been delivered at the ASC Conference in Los Angeles November 1, 2006.

[68] Author(s) unknown. "Becoming a Peer Reviewer for NIJ," National Institute of Justice, December 7, 2012, National Institute of Justice, Office of Justice Programs, Washington, D.C., http://www.nij.gov/nij/funding/reviews/peer-reviewers.htm.

[69] Damphousse, Kelly R., Ph.D. "Voice Stress Analysis: Only 15 Percent of Lies About Drug Use Detected in Field Test," March 17, 2008, NIJ Journal, National Institute of Justice, Office of Justice Programs, Washington, D.C., http://www.nij.gov/journals/259/voice-stress-analysis.htm.

[70] Author(s) unknown. "Guidelines Regarding Non-Competitive Awards," January 28, 2010, National Institute of Justice, Washington, D.C., http://www.nij.gov/nij/funding/reviews/non-competetive-awards.htm.

[71] "2011 NIJ Conference: Translational Criminology - Shaping Policy and Practice With Research," 2011 NIJ Conference, June 20-22, 2011, Arlington, Virginia, http://www.nij.gov/events/nij_conference/2011/welcome.htm.

[72] Lu, Natalie T. (National Institute of Justice, Washington, D.C.) and Taylor, Bruce G. (Caliber Associates, Fairfax, Virginia). "Drug screening and confirmation by GC–MS: Comparison of EMIT II and Online KIMS against 10 drugs between US and England laboratories," March 10, 2006, Forensic Science International, http://www.ncbi.nlm.nih.gov/pubmed/15899564.

[73] Oklahoma Secretary of State website,

http://www.sos.ok.gov/corp/corpInformation. Aspx?id=3500664556.

[74] Eriksson, Anders, and Lacerda, Francisco. "Charlatanry in forensic speech science: A problem to be taken seriously," December 2007, The International Journal of Speech, Language and the Law.

[75] Joyce, Janet, Managing Editor. "Note from Publisher," The International Journal of Speech, Language and the Law, December 4, 2008, http://www.equinoxjournals.com/index.php/IJSLL/article/viewArticle/3775.

[76] Author(s) unknown, "Study of the Utility and Validity of Voice Stress Analyzers," November 17, 2003, Virginia Board of Professional Regulations [known today as the Virginia Polygraph Examiners Advisory Board], Richmond, Virginia, http://www.dpor.virginia.gov/Boards/Polygraph-Examiners/.

[77] Haddad, Darren, et al. "INVESTIGATION AND EVALUATION OF VOICE STRESS ANALYSIS TECHNOLOGY, March 20, 2002, U.S. Department of Justice, Washington, D.C.

[78] Author(s) unknown, "TALKING PAPER ON SCREENING TEST FOR DETAINEE OPERATIONS," October 23, 2006, U.S. Air Force Polygraph Program, http://s3.documentcloud.org/documents/528234/fortishseven.txt.

[79] American Polygraph Association website, "Resources/Voice Stress - Review," January 24, 2013, http://www.polygraph.org/section/resources/review-voice-stress-based-technologies-detection-deception.

[80] Damphousse, Kelly R., Ph.D. "Voice Stress Analysis: Only 15 Percent of Lies About Drug Use Detected in Field Test," March 17, 2008, NIJ Journal, National Institute of Justice, Office of Justice Programs, Washington, D.C., http://www.nij.gov/journals/259/voice-stress-analysis.htm.

[81] Author(s) unknown, Army Field Manual 2-22.3, Human Intelligence Collector Operations, paragraph 13-7, September 2006, U.S. Army.

[82] Author(s) unknown, Army Field Manual 3-24, SECTION IV - COUNTERINTELLIGENCE AND COUNTERRECONNAISSANCE, paragraph 3-157, December 2006, U.S. Army.

[83] U.S. Senate Armed Services Committee Staff. "INQUIRY INTO THE TREATMENT OF DETAINEES IN U.S. CUSTODY," November 20, 2008, U.S. Senate Armed Services Committee, Washington, D.C.

[84] Bordin, Jeffrey, Ph.D. "A CRISIS OF TRUST AND CULTURAL

INCOMPATIBILITY: A Red Team Study of Mutual Perceptions of Afghan National Security Force Personnel and U.S. Soldiers in Understanding and Mitigating the Phenomena of ANSF-Committed Fratricide-Murders," May 12, 2011, International Security Assistance Force, Kabul Afghanistan.
[85] Author(s) unknown. "Report on Progress Toward Security and Stability in Afghanistan," December 10, 2012, Office of the Secretary of Defense, Washington, D.C., http://www.defense.gov/releases/release.aspx?releaseid=15730.
[86] News Release, "DOD Releases Report on Progress in Afghanistan," December 10, 2012, Office of the Secretary of Defense, Washington, D.C. http://www.defense.gov/releases/release.aspx?releaseid=15730.
[87] Author(s) unknown. "AFGHANISTAN: Key Oversight Issues (Report to Congressional Addressees, GOA-13-218SP), February 2013, U.S. Governmental Accountability Office, Washington, D.C.
[88] BORDERS, National Center for Border Security and Immigration, University of Arizona/Department of Homeland Security, http://borders.arizona.edu.
[89] Committee to Review the Scientific Evidence on the Polygraph, "The Polygraph and Lie Detection," 2003, National Research Council, Washington, D.C.
[90] Greenemeier, Larry. "Avatar Officer Installed at Arizona-Mexico Border, August 6, 2012, SCIENTIFIC AMERICAN™, http://scientificamerican.com/article.cfm?id=avatar-officer-installed-mexico-border.
[91] Lisaius, Som. "UA tech helps create cyber border," August 14, 2012, Tucson News Now, http://www.tucsonnewsnow.com/story/19269088/ua-tech-helps-create-cyber-border.
[92] National Association of Computer Voice Stress Analysts, http://nacvsa.org.
[93] Chapman, James L., and Stathis, Marigo. "Long-Term Retrospective Field Evaluation Of Voice Stress Analysis In A Criminal Justice Setting," December 2012, Criminalistics and Court Expertise (ISSN 0130-2655).
[94] Laessing, Ulf. "25 Saudi Guantanamo prisoners return to militancy," June 19, 2010, Reuters, http://www.reuters.com/article/idUSTRE65I22220100619.
[95] "CVSA" and "Computer Voice Stress Analyzer" are registered trademarks of National Institute for Truth Verification, 1100 Fortune Circle, West Palm

Beach, Florida, 33414. Last listed owner: Voice Biometrics, LLC, 16192 Coastal Highway, Lewes, Delaware 19958. Source: http://tess2.uspto.gov/bin/showfield?f=doc&state=4001:e28518.2.4.
[96] "VSA" and "Voice Stress Analysis" are registered trademarks of CCS Communications Control, Inc., 160 Midland Avenue, Port Chester, N.Y. 10573. Last listed owner: Homeland Security Strategies, Inc. 145 Huguenot Street, New Rochelle, N.Y. 10801. Source: http://tess2.uspto.gov/bin/showfield?f=doc&state=4007:o8myk4.4.38.

Made in the USA
Charleston, SC
21 September 2013